Praise for
Dog as My Doctor, Cat as My Nurse

"*Dog as My Doctor, Cat as My Nurse* is a beautifully written book filled with healing insights and heartwarming stories which compel us to look at our relationships with our dogs and cats in a whole new way. For those who seek out alternative therapies, or for those who are just curious, this engaging, informative, and entertaining read will have you marveling over the healing powers of dogs and cats. If you love animals you will love this book. If you don't live with an animal, you will want to adopt one so you too can live a healthier, happier, and more extraordinary life."

—MARIA JACQUEMETTON, Emmy Award-winning
Executive Producer and Writer, Mad Men

"Loved it! Everything that Carlyn shares in her book is the truth about the benefit of pets and your health. I know people who are alive today due to their pet's attitude, influence, and love. So read, learn, and get a pet!"

—BERNIE SIEGEL, MD, author of *Love, Animals & Miracles*,
and *A Book of Miracles*

"A truly masterful and inspiring work. Reading Carlyn's words felt as though I was embarking on a journey of healing wisdom from over the ages. Her powerful message for humans and their animal friends is a must read for all animal guardians if we are all to thrive in our modern world. It is a great honor and pleasure for me to recommend this absolutely wonderful book."

—ELLIOT M. KATZ, DVM, Founder and President Emeritus,
In Defense of Animals

"What an eye opener! Get ready to go on an insightful journey as Carlyn Montes De Oca reveals the unexpected healing powers of cats and dogs. An animal's ability to ⎸   ⎸ ⎸or real—it doesn't get any better than ⎸

—SHER ⎸ ‖‖‖‖‖‖‖‖‖‖‖‖‖‖‖‖‖‖‖ ⎸ Date.com,

T0125614

and Lovers

DOG as my DOCTOR,

CAT as my NURSE

An Animal Lover's Guide to a Healthy, Happy, and Extraordinary Life

CARLYN MONTES DE OCA L.Ac., M.T.O.M.

Illustrated by Giulia Notari

SHE WRITES PRESS

Published 2017
Printed in the United States of America
Print ISBN: 978-1-63152-186-7
E-ISBN: 978-1-63152-187-4
Library of Congress Control Number: 2016954983

For information, address:
She Writes Press
1563 Solano Ave #546
Berkeley, CA 94707

Cover design by Tabitha Lahr and Giulia Notari
Cover author photo © Michael Friel
Interior design © Tabitha Lahr
Illustrations by Giulia Notari

She Writes Press is a division of SparkPoint Studio, LLC.

This book is not intended as a substitute for the medical advice of physicians or veterinarians. The reader should regularly consult a physician in matters relating to his/her health and a veterinarian regarding their animal companion's health, particularly with respect to any symptoms that may require diagnosis or medical attention.

To my parents, whose greatest treasure were their children; to Ken, whose love reminds me that "para siempre" (forever) is not enough; and to my animal friends, who inspired this book . . . and who have never needed words to understand what lies in my heart.

CONTENTS

PART III: YOUR EXTRAORDINARY SPIRIT

INTRODUCTION

Your Journey Begins

"A best friend is like a four leaf clover, hard to find, lucky to have."

—Anonymous

If you are reading this book then you are probably in on a big secret known only to cat and dog lovers: our animal friends are *exceptional.*

Companionship, loyalty, and love are some of the priceless treasures that these beings bring into our lives. But even if you know this already, you may not be aware of one thing: your animal companions' greatest gift may lie in their ability to help you become healthier and happier, and to live life in a more extraordinary way.

If you have not yet discovered the connection between your well-being and your relationship with your animal friends, don't worry, you're not alone. It took me a lifetime of living with dogs, years of getting to know cats, and starting my own acupuncture and nutritional counseling business to begin to put two and two together.

When I opened my wellness practice, I began to notice how patients who were suffering from illnesses would break into smiles, burst out laughing, or just sigh with relief when sharing stories about their cats and dogs. Others patients with chronic pain frequently told me how they sought out their animals for solace and comfort. The more I heard these stories, the more I began to realize that cats and dogs, just by their unique way of being, deeply impact the lives of their human guardians in a positive and priceless way—that, in fact, they can actually make us healthier.

❊ ❊ ❊

As a practitioner of Chinese medicine, an acupuncturist, and a plant-based nutritional consultant in Northern California, I treat patients with chronic illnesses of all kinds, including heart disease, diabetes, arthritis, and cancer. The staggering truth is that "approximately 92% of older adults have at least one chronic disease, and 77% have at least two," according to the National Council on Aging, and "four of these diseases—heart disease, cancer, stroke, and diabetes—cause nearly two-thirds of all deaths each year."[1]

Are you a caretaker for an aging parent? Is your wife's face lined by worry or depression? Has your best friend just had a heart attack? Is your child being bullied because he is overweight? Are *you* the one suffering from a chronic illness?

Before you read any further, take a moment to assess where you are by asking yourself the following questions:

1. Am I as healthy as I want to be?
2. Do I wish I had more energy to do the things I love to do?
3. Do I often find myself stressed, worried, or sad?
4. Am I scared of getting older?
5. Am I afraid of dying?
6. Am I living my dream or just getting by in life?

And finally . . .

7. If my dog was my doctor or my cat was my nurse, and they held an important key to my health and happiness, would I be willing to follow their lead?

If you answered yes to any of these questions, and in particular the last one, then this book has been written especially for you!

Despite the medications and products we use to try to stay healthy and young, there is one essential element to enhancing our health that people rarely consider: *strengthening your connection to nature.*

For thousands of years, Chinese medicine has considered a connection to nature an integral part of our well-being. What you eat, the emotions you feel, and the lifestyle choices you make can either be in sync with nature or against her. But going against nature is never a win-win situation.

The thing is, if you are an animal lover, nature is not far removed from you. Our animal companions are nature's representatives. At this very moment your dog may be lying on your bed snuggled up beside you, her body comforting and warm and helping you relax after a challenging day. Or perhaps your cat is stretched across your stomach (an area that often feels tight from stress), mesmerizing you with his hypnotic purring. These are nature's healthy remedies brought to you by your cat and dog friends. This is their way of changing the world, one human at a time.

❖ ❖ ❖

I once had a six-pack. No, not the aluminum-can variety, or the ripples of muscle that some people have on their belly (though on this point I am eternally hopeful!). My "six-pack" was comprised of six animal companions—rescued cats and dogs whose friendship and wisdom enhanced my own health, added immensely to my happiness, and helped transform my spirit.

Let me introduce my motley crew:

1. **CODY** was a golden tabby we found hiding under a friend's house with his two brothers. We found homes for his siblings, but Cody insisted that his home was in my heart. The moment I looked into his green eyes, I agreed.

2. Years ago, my employer found a tuxedo kitty wandering through the streets of Hollywood. **JESTER** stayed at our office during the week until we eventually found him a forever home: on my bed in my apartment.

3. **DAKOTA** is a black chow who we rescued from a shelter as a puppy. We joke that she was a bribe to my stepkids so they wouldn't run away from home when they found out they had to move to Los Angeles (bribes work!).

4. I met **ROXY** when the police brought her into a high-kill shelter after her guardians were arrested for selling drugs. Roxy was a tough street dog, but the moment she put her paw over my hand, I knew our connection was for life.

5. When my friend Theresa adopted a dog from a shelter who turned out to be pregnant, the look in Theresa's eyes told me I had better take one of the puppies when they were born or else! That's is how **RUDY,** a chocolate lab mix, joined our growing family.

6. And finally there was **TEDDY,** our senior citizen, who was found on skid row looking more like a dingy floor mop than a dog. After several baths and a lot of love, Teddy turned out to be a loyal, affectionate, gentle chow chow, and a valued member of our family.

So, how did four dogs and two cats inspire me to spend five years writing a book? Simple: As I started to pay attention, I began to notice all of the amazing and subtle ways these creatures had of supporting my physical health and emotional happiness. When I was going through the pangs of my divorce, feeling lonely and sad, Jester would find his way onto my chest and lay across it, as if he was absorbing the pain in my heart. His mere presence and eventual purring soothed me like nothing else could. Roxy and her keen nose, meanwhile, always seemed to know when it was time for me to de-stress for the day; just when I was getting wound up, I'd find her chin on my lap and her eyes staring into mine as if to say, "How about a walk?" And no matter what mood I was in, Teddy could always make me laugh as he pranced around the living room. Teddy seemed to know how not to sweat the small stuff, even when in later days, the "small stuff" was death.

My six-pack has enriched my life beyond measure. As you read the upcoming chapters and allow our experiences into your heart, I hope they enrich your life too.

❊ ❊ ❊

Here's how this is going to work. This book is comprised into three major sections:

1. Your Healthy Body
2. Your Happy Mind
3. Your Extraordinary Spirit

Within each chapter you will find:

- Animal-inspired keys to greater health and how you can best utilize them.
- Poignant stories from animal lovers whose bond with their four-legged friends have brought them greater health, happiness, and purpose.
- My own personal stories, inspired by my lively six-pack.
- Advice, interviews, and stories from extraordinary people— including New York Times best-selling author Jack Canfield, cat behaviorist and television show host Jackson Galaxy, television journalist Jane Velez-Mitchell and Ingrid Newkirk, president of People for the Ethical Treatment of Animals—who are changing the world because their minds were inspired, and their hearts touched, by their bonds with their animal friends.
- A wrap-up of the chapter with action steps prescribed by Nurse Kitty Wiskas and Dr. Harry Friend.

By the end of our journey together, you will take away three things:

1. Secrets for greater health and well-being
2. An enhanced awareness of your connection to nature
3. A more meaningful, enriching, and deeper relationship with your animal companions . . . and yourself.

For your viewing pleasure, go to the *Dog as My Doctor, Cat as My Nurse* online photo gallery: www.AnimalHumanHealth.com/gallery. The gallery contains pictures of the many characters you will encounter on the pages to come (both the two- and four-legged variety). I recommend visiting the photo gallery after you finish reading each chapter; it will add to your animal–human health connection experience.

(*A final note regarding the title of this book:* I love cats and dogs and hold the two species in equal regard. Selecting a cat as a nurse and a dog as a doctor is really more about creative license than feeling one medical profession or animal species is better than the other. The truth is, I needed a book title, and "Dog as My Doctor" came to me as I was walking my dog Roxy. "Cat as My Nurse" popped into my head a few minutes later while I was napping with my cat, Jester.)

❋ ❋ ❋

We animal lovers are a mighty crew, and I am humbled and honored to be part of this community. Animal lovers go to great lengths to help our four-legged friends. We endure the judgments of those who don't understand our commitment to animals, and we hurt deeply when we see them mistreated. When animal guardians are fortunate enough to connect with one another, we form a kinship based on a deep understanding that all animals are worthy of love and respect, and that we are better humans because of them.

This awareness of the healing potential of our animal friends could not come at a better time. Individually and collectively, we are at a precipice of a new age—a crossroads of a global awakening. Our planet is experiencing a tremendous paradigm shift, a changing of the old guard. The antiquated mode of thinking that has led to a depletion of our resources, an accumulation of toxicity, and a disregard for Mother Nature is now being challenged. The threats to our survival that we now face are forcing us to realize that the only way out of this mire is through collaboration with each other, regardless of our species. But to heal and transform *The Whole*, we must begin by transforming *The One*, and ultimately that means transforming ourselves.

Every day, and in everything that we do, we have the power to choose. We can choose to make lifestyle choices that bring us to chronic illness, or instead, we can choose wellness. If we choose the path of wellness, remember that as animal lovers, we do not walk alone; our companions are on this ride with us. They can help us transform our lives for the better; all we have to do is allow it.

Just like any great road trip, the journey toward our best health can be a joyous one, especially when you realize that you are in the company of angels. Because those of us who love animals can see them as no less.

PART I

Your Healthy Body

If a dog were my doctor or a cat my nurse,
what advice would they give me?

*"Every day you must stretch, shake your booty, let people see how
totally excited you are to be around them, pointedly demand food
when you're hungry, and live rapturously in the moment."*

—Jane Velez Mitchell, television journalist and author

CHAPTER 1

Super Dog and Mighty Cat

"Thou art the Great Cat, the avenger of the Gods, and the judge of words, and the president of the sovereign chiefs and the governor of the holy Circle; thou art indeed . . . the Great Cat."

—Inscription on the Royal Tombs at Thebes

Batman, Spiderman, Wolverine, and Aquaman—four out of the top ten superheroes listed in a *Parade Magazine* survey are named after animals or aspects of nature. Throughout time and across cultures, we humans have marveled at the special powers of animals. The strength of bears, the courage of lions, the grace of eagles—all of these qualities stir our imaginations and touch our souls.

Our own animal companions may not have Aquaman's power to swim as fast as dolphins or Spiderman's ability to scale skyscrapers, but they do have some unique powers of their own when it comes to enhancing our well-being and longevity. With chronic disease currently presenting itself as our greatest "health villain," we have never needed their aid as badly as we do today.

Do you know your cat's or dog's superpowers? If not, let me share five of them with you now:

1. PETTING

Petting is the most well-known cat and dog superpower. Researchers have studied petting, and their conclusions are unanimous: petting your cats and dogs is great for your heart and blood pressure, and will even give your immune system a boost.[2],[3] When we calmly engage in petting, our bodies release oxytocin, the "love hormone." When oxytocin gets activated, stress starts to melt away, and we feel better about ourselves, our life, and those around us.

But wait, there's more! Petting your beloved friends can also increase your theta brain waves. This brain activity is not only associated with greater relaxation but with bringing us into a heightened state of intuition, helping us remember long lost memories and inspiring our creativity.[4]

If you have a four-legged friend, you may already know how good it feels to stroke your dog's coat or feel the silky sweetness of a cat's fur under your fingertips. Or perhaps it is they who have already trained *you* to pet *them* on demand when they jump on your lap or when they lay their muzzle on your knee. And petting is not just good for your health; it benefits your animal's health as well. (Only when they agree to it, of course. After all, this is a health partnership.)

The next time you have a tough day at work or are feeling a little blue, instead of reaching for a drink, a candy bar, or an aspirin, you might want to reach out to your feline or canine friend instead. If they are urging you to pet them, go for it! It will be good for both of you.

2. PLACEMENT

Have you ever noticed that cats seem to have an uncanny knack for finding an injury, pain, or discomfort on your body, and then lying across the area in question as if trying to soothe the pain?

My cat Cody liked to lie near my upper back, where I have a curvature in my spine. Jester, my tuxedo tabby, instead preferred to lie on my lower back, where I have degeneration in a disc. It's as if they had a powwow and decided who was in charge of helping the different parts of my back to heal. The solid pressure of Jester's warm, big-boned body on my spine, combined with his hypnotic purring, provided me with a soothing relief that often sent me into a deep sleep: a welcome respite after a long day at work.

Many years ago, Lani, a Hawaiian health care professional, told me that when she was a child, whenever she or one of her siblings came down with a stomachache, her aunties would place a kitten across their belly. The aunties believed that the cat could absorb the negative energy, like a poultice, and make the child well again.

Superstition? Old wives' tales? The truth is, the specifics don't really matter when you're sick. Whether the "illness" is actually absorbed by the cat or the comfort of having a warm fuzzy body to cuddle with is what does the trick, when you're in pain, all you want to do is to feel better again. According to Lani, Cat Belly Therapy makes that happen.

Cats aren't the only ones who have this placement thing mastered. Studies have shown that Xolos (Mexican hairless dogs) generate intense heat from their bodies—far more than the average cat or dog.[5] For people suffering from fibromyalgia, a debilitating disease that causes unrelenting muscle pain, Xolos make great companions because their pain can be relieved by heat. And bonding with a Xolo also has more than just physical benefits: our Xolo friends can also offer much-needed comfort to a fibro patient who also may be contending with depression and anxiety (ailments that often accompany this disease).

3. PURRING

If you are fortunate enough to live with a cat, you know something that a dog lover might not: that a cat's meow is in their *purr*. I've found that lying in bed with my cats, stroking their plush fur, and listening to their purrfect resonance is one of the most pleasurable and soothing activities life has to offer.

Most people assume that cats purr because they are happy or content, but that's not the whole story. Yes, feeling relaxed is one of the reasons cats purr; however, they also purr when they are injured, stressed, or giving birth. And they purr to heal.

There is an old veterinary saying that goes, "If you put a cat and a bunch of broken bones in the same room, the bones will heal." What we've learned is that when it comes to healing, a cat's purr goes beyond the sound; it's about vibration. Scientists from the Institute of Fauna in North Carolina tell us that the vibration in a cat's purr falls between 20 and 140 Hz. This range helps accelerate bone growth, heal fractures, and relieve pain, and can also repair tendons and muscles.[6] These techniques have been employed in sports medicine to help athletes rehabilitate faster. Right now, the feline friend strewn across your legs is purring at these very same frequencies.

In a medical article in the *New Zealand Veterinary Journal*, scientist T. F. Cook related how he discovered the curative effects that purring had on a six-year-old male Siamese cat with an acute respiratory tract infection.[7] At the beginning of the experiment, the cat's eyes were nearly swollen shut, his nasal cavities were almost completely blocked, and his breathing was extremely labored. The cat was so depleted and weak that euthanasia was being considered. But Cook found that when the cat began to purr, his breathing became easier, and the more he purred, the better he got. The next day, the kitty began to eat, and twenty-four hours later, his breathing went back to normal.

Cats' purrs can help calm our nerves. They even soothe tension headaches, according to several of my own cat guardian patients. So if you are fortunate enough to live with a cat, remember: the quality time you spend interacting with them can be therapeutic for both of you. Just ask Christine Kloser, an award-winning author and book coach whose guidance has transformed the lives of visionary entrepreneurs and authors around the world; if you do, she's sure to tell you about a cat named Schumper.

Schumper & Christine

"Schumper" is a made-up word that my husband and I created before our cat ever came into our lives. When we adopted him from the ASPCA he was named Scoobie Doo. But within seventy-two hours of bringing him home, it was clear that he was not a Scoobie Doo but a Schumper instead.

Schumper is my guardian angel and he helps me stay connected to my soul. If I'm having a tough day, feeling stressed out, or working too hard, he reminds me that it's time to take a break by jumping on my keyboard or sit-

ting on my lap (the way he is right now). Sometimes he crawls up my chest so his chin is near my face, nudges me, or paces back and forth across my desk. Schumper will try just about anything to make his presence known. Lounging on the sofa and keeping me company is Schumper's simple way of bringing me back into balance. We are so connected, he and I.

Schumper influences my creativity by reminding me to shift from doing-ness into being-ness. He is a great example of living in that space. The times when I stop to sit and pet him are all about just being. His purr is an instant connection to the magnificence of life, and it quells my thinking mind. Once, when I was away for several days and feeling stressed, my husband and daughter taped Schumper purring and e-mailed the file to me because they know how grounding that sound is for me.

I can't help but think, what would the world be like if everyone just purred? That feeling it gives you—ahhhh, all is well, life is good, I love you— is unbeatable. If the world could just purr we would all heal, and find peace.

---

4. POWER NOSES

Recently my stepdaughter, Gina, visited us from college. One night, as she lay on the floor, the dogs piled on top of her. Laughing, she lifted her head out from beneath the jumble of fur and told me that Dakota would not stop licking her ankle. Gina was on the ultimate Frisbee team at her school, and she had twisted her ankle during a game. Now it was swollen and tender and Dr. Dakota was methodically licking it, clearly aware something was not right on her foot.

"Licking your wounds" is a saying for a reason; studies show that dog saliva contains histatins, chemicals that can help a wound heal from infection faster.[8]

When you have several animals at home, like I do, their licking of each other can alert you to an injury or problem that you might not have otherwise noticed. In this way, they become each other's doctors and nurses.

Dakota's tongue may not have healed Gina's swollen ankle, but Gina's laughter got her mind off of her injury for a while, and it gave her body a good dose of the positive hormones that accompany laughter. But how did Dakota know to administer the licking and the laughter therapy? She used her nose to sniff out what was amiss.

Canines and felines experience a large part of their world through their snouts. Their sense of smell is generally 10,000–100,000 times stronger than a human being's.

Their nose *knows*. In recent years, cats and dogs have been using their nasal superpowers to alert epileptics before and after oncoming seizures, and to warn their guardians of potential heart attacks.

At the Pine Street Acupuncture Clinic in San Anselmo, California, doctors Michael McCullogh and Michael Broffman have been conducting research for the last twenty years on dogs' ability to detect cancer through their sense of smell. During trials, canine participants are taught to smell out ovarian, lung, and breast cancer. When they detect the disease in a breath sample vial, they sit in front of it to alert their handlers. Sometimes, however, that unhealthy sample is not a vial but an actual human being.

Dr. McCullough shared a story with me about what happened when the guardian of one of the dogs who had participated in the trials took him to a dog show to compete:

> *Normally dogs receive the prize ribbon for demonstrating their award-winning posture and gait—but in the middle of the show, this dog suddenly sat down, rather somberly, at the feet of one of the judges. In our training at the clinic, the dogs sit down when they smell something amiss; when what they smell is cancer. After conferring with the dog's handler and realizing why the dog was sitting down in front of her and what it might mean, the judge decided to heed the dog's alert and went to see her doctor. The diagnosis was as the dog had indicated: she had cancer.*
>
> *It's remarkable that the dog did this in a totally different context, in a totally different location, with a new person, and even with a type of cancer that the dog had not even been trained to detect. It goes to show that dogs know more about your health than you know about theirs. You have to take your dog to a vet to find out what is wrong with them, but your*

dog already knows what is going on with you. The first step, therefore, should not be to wait and see what our dogs can do for us when it comes to our health but to find out what your dog already knows that you haven't yet noticed. All of the little signals they give you—the tugging on your leg, the barking, the whining—this could be the dog saying, "You don't look so good today" or "A little sunshine would do you wonders" or "Are you sure you want to talk to her that way?" If you pay attention and look closely, your dog is already doing his or her job.

5. PERSONAL MIRRORING

As a child I was entertained, delighted, and inspired by movies—so as an adult, to work on films as an editor and get paid for it was a dream come true. What I didn't realize, though, was that the movie business could be a far too demanding mistress. Epic hours, paired with the taxing personalities I sometimes worked with, could send my stress levels skyrocketing. This lethal combination would sometimes cause my back to suddenly spasm to the point where even breathing would become excruciating.

Relief came through acupuncture, administered by the skillful hands of Dr. Mikio Sankey. As I lay on his treatment table, Mikio would gently insert tiny needles into different parts of my body, providing almost instant pain relief.

Like you do with a hairdresser, you tend to tell your acupuncturist pretty much everything. During the course of my conversations with Mikio, I told him about Cody, my golden tabby cat, and how he insisted on lying across my back, right near the curvature in my spine.

"What do you think Cody is trying to tell you?" Mikio asked.

"No idea," I said.

"Animals often try to tell us something we need to know about ourselves," he told me. "You just have to be willing to hear it."

They say that in time our animals reflect our physical appearance, and that may be, but what Mikio was suggesting, and what other experts are now backing up, is that this mirroring goes beyond hair style, body type, or facial features.[9] Take a moment to think about how your cat or dog might reflect something about your overall health. Is your dog overweight? If so, are you or is someone else in your family carrying a few extra pounds? Is your cat acting agitated, stressed, or anxious? Perhaps you've been working a few too many hours each day and need to take some time to unwind and relax.

In my years of clinical experience, I've observed that a patient's physical problems usually have a deeper root than the obvious physical symptoms. A profound blow to our emotions can eventually manifest in headaches, back pain, and gut issues. Perhaps you have felt yourself get angry or anxious, only to have your stomach react in painful knots. With their keen senses and heightened awareness, our animal companions can sense our emotions—often before we do. So pay attention to how your cat or dog reflects your own health; it will not only give you a new, insightful, and powerful tool to add to your health kit, it will also create an opportunity for a deeper connection between you and your best friend.

PARTNERSHIP: *YOUR* SUPERPOWER!

Petting, Placement, Purring, Power Noses, and Personal Mirrors—these are just five of the superpowers that allow cats and dogs to guide their humans toward a healthier, happier, and more extraordinary life. But to maximize the effects of any of your companion's superpowers, you will need to activate your end of the animal-human bond by employing your own superpower: Partnership.

Scientific American reports that the healing benefits of animals take place when they and their guardian are emotionally connected[10]—which makes it extra important to strengthen your bond with your animal friends by nurturing your "ships" with them: your relation*ship*, your friend*ship*, and your guardian*ship*. In this way, your partner*ship* will blossom and reward you in ways that you cannot imagine.

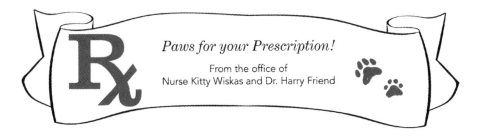

1. Now that we've revealed our superpowers to you, why not enjoy them with us?

2. If we get sick, please take us to see our own doctors and nurses. Once we're taken care of, take the opportunity to see if your own physical health needs attention.

3. If we are misbehaving and you're not sure why, don't just get mad at us. Take time to look in the mirror and you might discover something about the person who is staring back.

COMING UP: Oh what a glorious morning, oh what a splendid day . . . What, you don't feel glorious or splendid until after you've had a large cup of coffee? Well then, a morning ritual may just be what your dog doctor or cat nurse has in store for you!

CHAPTER 2

Your Morning Ritual

*"We give dogs time we can spare, space
we can spare, and love we can spare.
And in return, dogs give us their all.
It's the best deal man has ever made."*

—M. Facklam

If you are interested in living a healthy, happy, and truly extraordinary life, you shouldn't even *consider* facing the world first thing in the morning without engaging in a morning ritual. Don't worry, I'm not talking about human sacrifices and primal dancing. I'm merely suggesting activities like meditation, breathing exercises, listening to inspirational podcasts, enjoying music, reading uplifting books, practicing tai chi, saying affirmations, doing yoga, or writing in a journal. Got something else in mind? Great! As long as it is positive, nurturing, and empowering, it can become part of your daily morning routine.

THESE MAGIC MOMENTS

Our brains produce different brainwaves throughout the day depending on our moods, activities, and state of mind. When you first wake up in the morning, your brain waves are in an alpha state, relaxed but effortlessly alert (alpha waves are the bridge between your conscious and subconscious mind). Because of this, the moments just after you wake are when you are most susceptible to "light bulb" ideas, new thoughts, and increased creativity. It is a common time to remember where you left your keys, to flash on that name you completely forgot, or to come up with a great ending for your book. Top athletes compete more optimally when their brains produce more alpha waves, and Navy Seals are trained to enter alpha states to reduce their stress levels and help them make better decisions.[11], [12]

5 BENEFITS OF A MORNING RITUAL

- Calms and relaxes you, and sets you up for the rest of the day
- Enhances memory
- Benefits creativity
- Improves problem-solving abilities
- Increases learning capabilities

Because your mind is so malleable in the early A.M., it is the worst time for you to plop out of bed and fill your head with disturbing news events that may come over cyberspace. The more stressed we get, the more we become susceptible to life's curveballs, as well as the stress-related disorders that lie at the root of many illnesses.

For many years I did not have a morning ritual in place. Looking back, it's no wonder that I felt I had no control over my life or moods, and blamed the things that happened to me on circumstances or other people. Now that I've incorporated a morning ritual into my day, I have the clarity to see that *I* am the master of my day. I may not be able to control the moment-to-moment life challenges I encounter, but I can control how I feel when I first wake up; I can plant my interior garden with enthusiasm, optimism, and confidence, or I can allow it to run wild with insecurity, fear, and irritation. The choice is ultimately mine.

A morning ritual feels great and the benefits are tremendous. And the best part is, if you have animal friends, you can add them to your morning ritual to sweeten the deal even more!

If you need some convincing on this point, read what Bob has to say about how his cat, Jordan's insistence on enjoying a morning ritual changed his life.

Jordan & Bob

Twelve years ago, my wife, Mary, found a tiny silver and grey kitten under a dumpster at a construction site. She brought the kitty home and we named her Jordan.

I get up early in the morning, well before Mary does. Because it is very quiet and Zen-like at that time of day, this is when I engage in my morning rituals. Washing the dishes, feeding our bird, and making a latte for my wife are some of the things I enjoy doing. I have a business helping people with highly stressful tax issues, and the morning is my quiet time to get my thoughts together for the rest of the day.

From the first day we brought her home, as soon as she heard me stir in the morning, Jordan would stretch her body then rub against my legs, wanting me to scratch her back and gently pull on her tail. Filling her food bowl and opening her cat door wasn't enough for her; Jordan wanted me to interact with her even more. As I washed the dishes, she would roll over onto her back to distract me and try get me to play with her . . . which I often did.

Although I loved my time with Jordan, there were days when I got really busy and had to get to work early. I'd get so wrapped up in my thoughts that not only would I ignore Jordan, I would stomp around the house from room to room, unaware of the noise I was making.

"Bob, you're scaring Jordan!" Mary would yell.

Realizing that I could step on Jordan and accidentally hurt her always brought my thoughts back to the present—which is a great place to be. To have this lovely little creature be there for me every morning, so happy to see me wake up, gave me a warm and loving feeling.

When Jordan turned eleven, she began to have trouble walking. She was in pain, stopped eating, and the quality of her life began to diminish.

After a visit to the vet, Mary told me, "Bob, it's time. We have to let her go."

I refused and told her I wasn't ready. But Mary made me see that this decision was not about me. I had to find the strength to do what was best for Jordan. And I did.

The last morning Jordan and I were together, I got up extra early and spent as much time with her as I could. I even came home early to have a picnic with her. Outside in the sunshine, Mary and I fed Jordan her favorite foods and let her know we loved her. I know she enjoyed those hours, being in the sunlight with us.

Then the vet came and we had to say good-bye.

Over the next few weeks, my morning ritual was no longer filled with the joy I had experienced for so many years. I realized how frivolous and stupid it was to leave early for work when I didn't have to, or how I would get distracted by meaningless events instead of enjoying Jordan and my family. Jordan is gone, but she taught me how important this is. And I'm different now because of her.

Today we have a new cat living with us—Juno. Juno gets as much quality time with me as she wants every morning, and this is directly because of Jordan. We are a family, my wife, Juno, and me, and I value every moment we have together.

MY SIX-PACK IN THE WEE HOURS

"If a patient comes into your office and they are so sick that you have no idea what to do for them . . . teach them to breathe." This is what a master teacher taught me in Chinese Medical School.

Breathing is a key to life. In our fast-paced world, most of us breathe shallowly, as if we are in some kind of peril, instead of breathing more deeply, which aids with relaxation. Deep breathing can help us restore our body, diminish our stress, and ease our thoughts. And while you can breathe deeply and mindfully anywhere and at any time, the very best time to take in those long, deep, detoxifying breaths is first thing in the morning.

The youngest member of my pack, Rudy, has a sizeable snout—not unlike a certain red-nosed reindeer. Rudy's deep breathing and snoring serves as a great reminder that I shouldn't get out of bed until I've taken a few long, deep breaths myself.

When they sensed I was awake (and sometimes when I was still asleep), my cats Cody and Jester always liked to begin their own morning rituals around me by gracefully bending their backs and creating healthy spaces between each of their vertebrae. Meanwhile, Roxy, our self-appointed alpha dog, would see the cats up and steal the limelight by engaging in her own yoga version of "downward dog." Watching my cats and dogs was a good reminder that I needed to stretch my own back after a long night's sleep.

If my mind drifted to thoughts about the phone calls I had to make and the e-mails I needed to return, the feeling of Dakota's warm tongue gently licking my hand would distract me. When she finished grooming me, her gentle face and sweet smile would remind me that I had forgotten a very important part of my morning ritual: the practice of gratitude.

GRATITUDE 101

As you wake up from your night's sleep, let two words—*thank you*—be the first conscious thought to form in your mind. Because your alpha brain waves are strongest at this time, giving thanks each morning can have a profoundly positive impact on your day. Express gratitude for the large things in your life, such as your health, your relationships, and the fact of being alive; but express it for the small things as well—the hummingbird buzzing outside your window, the memory of the funny thing your child said yesterday, or the smile you received from someone you didn't even know. These may seem like relatively inconsequential moments, but expressing gratitude for them will not only impact your attitude, it will affect your health.

Research has shown that when we show gratitude for just three things every day, we get a measurable boost in happiness. Jon Gordon, who cites this study in his book *The No Complaining Rule*, further says that it's physiologically impossible to be stressed and thankful at the same time because two thoughts can't occupy your brain simultaneously.[13] If you are focusing on gratitude, it's going to be pretty hard to be negative.

5 WAYS GRATITUDE TRANSFORMS YOUR BODY

- Releases nitric oxide, the "happy gas" that benefits immunity
- Relaxes the body and eases stress
- Helps balance your reactions to outside influences
- Boosts your immune system
- Helps create a more positive attitude

Gratitude practice is simple, though it may not seem that way if you are currently feeling tested by life. When unexpected events slap us in the face and we're head-to-head with an emotional tsunami, it's hard to say "Thank you." But if you begin your practice ahead of the storm, when your emotional waters are less turbulent, your reserves will grow, making it easier for you to call on them when the tempest is most challenging.

But what if you just don't feel grateful? My advice is to look to your animal friends. Our cats and dogs—especially those that have been rescued from difficult situations—often model gratitude quite well. The wagging tails when you give them the slightest affection, their silly antics when you take a few minutes to play, their enthusiastic barking or purring when you come home . . . our animal friends exude gratitude even for the smallest things. Consider animals your gratitude buddies, waiting and eager to show you the way.

Teddy, my chow, taught me a profound lesson in gratitude, one that I have never forgotten.

Teddy & Carlyn

Rescuers in Los Angeles's Skid Row spotted a filthy, mop-like creature hungrily rifling through overturned garbage cans. For two days he eluded his captors, but on the third day they were able to lure him with food and rescue him. After an unappreciated bath, the caked mud disappeared down the drain, revealing an old black chow chow underneath.

Teddy was fiercely independent, snapped at anyone who approached him, and kept to himself. In quick order, his rescuers decided he was a liability and should be euthanized. "Look at him," one of them said to me. "Who's ever going to want him?"

I will admit that Teddy was a bit of a mess. Even after his bath, his hair remained matted and he was no spring chicken either. According to the vet, Teddy was at least ten years old. The rescue organization felt that because he was aggressive, he was also unadoptable. I understood their concerns, but still, I never quite saw the impossibility that they saw. I looked at the rescue owner and said, "I want him."

It was a bad idea, I was told; I already had three dogs and two cats living with me, I was a new wife and stepmom to two kids, and I had just opened my acupuncture practice. I was busy, busy, busy . . . but the spark of hope behind Teddy's gentle brown eyes was something I could not turn away from; my gut told me that all this boy needed was a second chance. I was determined to give it to him, so I brought him home.

Teddy looked liked a bear—and he acted like an unhappy one. Exposed nerves inside of his mouth, an abscess on the side of his face, a tooth in need of a root canal . . . it's no wonder Teddy was so distressed. A human with any one of these conditions would be in incredible pain, explained the kind vet. Once Teddy's mouth healed and his pain dissipated, the "vicious" chow chow transformed into the sweetest, most loyal, and grateful companion anyone could wish for.

In the ensuing years, it became clear to me that Teddy never took his life with us for granted. He seemed grateful for everything he had—his warm bed, the wholesome food we fed him, and the love we gave him every day. He often pranced around the house like a little pony after he was given a stuffed toy or treat, or even just a kiss on his furry head.

We enjoyed our lives together until he passed away. And even in his final days, when I would carry him to his bed or out for a sunbath, Teddy would lick my hand and look into my eyes, and I could feel his gratitude so powerfully that it makes me cry to remember it now.

From Teddy and all my animal companions, I have learned the power of gratitude. Because as grateful as Teddy was to be part of our lives, and to be given a second chance, there could be no one more grateful to have known him, cared for him, and witnessed his redemption than me.

Paws for your Prescription!

From the office of
Nurse Kitty Wiskas and Dr. Harry Friend

1. Start your day with a morning ritual each and every morning.

2. Not sure what your morning ritual should look like? How about spending five quality minutes with your favorite four-legged gratitude buddy? This is a great time to nurture our partnership, cement our allegiance, and scratch our ears.

3. Make your morning ritual a nighttime ritual too! You will reap the rewards twice as fast.

COMING UP: Now that you have your morning ritual in hand, it's time to head to the kitchen!

CHAPTER 3

The New Taste of Nutrition

"I've met many thinkers and many cats, but the wisdom of cats is infinitely superior."

—Hippolyte Taine

What would happen if you filled a Maserati's gas tank with diesel instead of premium fuel? What if you watered your garden with bourbon instead of water? What if you fed a lion a diet of potato chips? The car would tank out, your garden would wilt, and the poor lion . . . well, you get the picture.

Food is medicine; it can help you combat disease, maintain great health, and add years to your life. Yet most Americans eat a diet that does the opposite. If you are the average American, you are probably consuming white flour products, excess alcohol, and 130 pounds of refined sugar a year.[14] If this is your MO, then you are on the Standard American Diet—or SAD, as this diet is often called.

Unfortunately, our cats and dogs have been doing the SAD thing right alongside of us. As our reliance on packaged cat and dog foods has increased, our animal companions have begun to come down with more degenerative diseases than ever before.[15]

I don't blame you if you get frustrated by how hard it is to determine what foods you and your family should eat to live long and healthy lives. There are countless theories, studies, and experts telling us what to do.

But the truth is, unless you have a health condition that requires a particular protocol, nutrition doesn't have to be complicated. Sometimes it is a matter of committing to the basics instead of leap-frogging over them in search of the latest and greatest. Here are some nutrition essentials to get you started on the right path—inspired by our animal friends, of course!

1. EAT WHOLE FOODS

When I was growing up, we fed our dogs cheap processed food. It was convenient and fast, and truthfully, we didn't know any better. I now feel a deep pang of regret knowing that my friends' lives may have been shortened because they were deprived of the level of nutrition they needed. Today, the quality of processed pet foods may be better than it was thirty years ago, but even high-quality packaged food is no match for fresh whole foods.

Not everyone has the time or can afford to eat fresh, whole, or organic 24/7, but people who focus on feeding wholesome foods to their cats and dogs often adhere to the same standards for themselves. And when we give ourselves *and* our companions the most nourishing foods we can afford, it helps us both build stronger bodies and the potential for a longer life—together.

The next time you rip open a bag of food for your cat or dog, and a few minutes later tear open a box of macaroni and cheese for you, take pause: maybe you could both benefit from a baked sweet potato instead.

2. WATER IS THE ELIXIR OF LIFE

Dogs drink water with vigor, cats with a delicate grace. Whichever approach *your* drinking style resembles, remember: when you spot your companions lapping from their water bowls, it's a great reminder for you to grab a glass of water, too.

Approximately 60 percent of our body consists of water, yet many of us are regularly dehydrated.[16] Headaches, body aches, fatigue, dry skin, weight gain, loss of concentration—these are just some of the symptoms that can arise from a lack of water.

How much water do you need every day? It varies; everyone is different, and your environment plays a part as well. In the winter you can drink less than during the summer, when you are sweating more. If you are an athlete or exercise a lot, you will need more water to replenish the liquid you've lost than someone less active would. The following is a great little formula to approximate how much water to drink per day.

Basic Water Formula
Drink ½ your body weight in ounces.
(e.g., If you weigh 120 pounds then you require 60 ounces of water daily.)

Keeping hydrated is important. Use your animal sense, and listen to what your body needs.

3. CHOOSE YOUR HUMAN TREATS WELL

If you're lucky enough to live with a dog, then you're probably familiar with *treat time*. "Sit," "Stay," or "Give me a kiss" may seem like a lot of work for a mere sweet potato tidbit, but these moments are fun. They're also a great way for you and your friends to learn to communicate better with each other, which can strengthen your bond with one another.

For humans, eating healthy treats can also bring rewards, especially when it comes to balancing your blood sugar levels—a key factor in managing your weight, reducing food cravings, and sustaining your energy throughout the day. Eating nutritious snacks between meals will prevent you from getting too hungry, which will make you less tired and less cranky. If you don't get enough fruits and vegetables in your diet, eating them between breakfast, lunch and dinner is a great way to do it.

One thing to note: Recent studies reveal that given a choice, canines will choose love as a reward from their guardians over treats.[17] Humans cannot live by bread alone, and maybe we can learn something here from our dogs and allow love instead of food to fill our bellies from time to time.

4. IT PAYS TO BE FINICKY

Have you ever prepared a tiny feast for your feline friend, only to have them turn their nose skyward and walk away from their bowl with disdain? Rejection hurts. But maybe there is something here that humans can learn from cats.

Being finicky like a cat can be beneficial when it comes to making a choice between a cup of coffee and a glass of lemon water, or between the bag of chips and the handful of blueberries. Besides that, your stomach is only approximately as large as your fist. Think of the amount of food you are putting into it at every meal. Is it two fist sizes? Three? Would you benefit from eating smaller portions, like Cody, my sleek twenty-year-old tabby, who only ate when he was hungry?

Like a cat, be curious about your food. Try something new and fun. Explore tastes, smells, and textures that you may not have tried before. But also remember that when it comes to ensuring your own longevity, being a little finicky can be make all the difference.

5. DINE WITH AN ATTITUDE OF GRATITUDE

When I was growing up, my family always said grace at the dinner table before we ate.

These days, I don't say grace anymore. Instead, my meals are eaten quickly, usually on the go, and sadly, without much gratitude.

My dogs, on the other hand, are full of gratitude. When I put their food down for them, they act as though they've just received the greatest gift I could have ever given them. After he's licked his bowl clean, Rudy doesn't contain his joy. He runs into the living room, leaps onto his bed, and flops onto his back, belly-up like a beetle. Gravity pulls the corners of his lips into a wide, goofy grin while his tail thumps back and forth like a metronome.

Dogs bring their hearts into everything they do, even eating. We can do the same. Or, if you prefer to be like Jester, my tuxedo cat, you can show your gratitude in a more demure and graceful way, as he did by licking his paws with satisfaction.

Now that you have these five animal-inspired nutritional nuggets in your front pocket, you are ready to delve into Mother Nature's New Taste of Nutrition: the whole foods, plant-based diet.

WHOLE FOODS, PLANT-BASED NUTRITION

What if your breakfasts, lunches, and dinners were nutritious, delicious and also . . .

- gave you more energy and vitality
- helped you drop weight and keep it off
- lessened the cost of your medical bills
- had a profoundly positive impact on the environment
- decreased animal suffering

You can do all of these things for yourself when you adopt a whole foods, plant-based diet. It consists of a variety of delicious and nutritious whole foods, such as fruits, vegetables, nuts, legumes, and grains. What it leaves out are animal proteins, such as meat, dairy, and eggs.

"*Hmmm, no meat?*" I hear you saying. "*But haven't humans been eating meat since the beginning of time? Weren't our ancestors hunters? What about the Paleo diet?*" Well, let's defer to Mother Nature, some experts, and our own anatomy for clues.

THE EXPERTS WEIGH IN

Neal Barnard, M.D., is the president of Physicians Committee for Responsible Medicine (PCRM), an organization focused on science-based research for promoting optimal health. He is also the author of numerous books on nutrition. Dr. Barnard had a lot to say during our interview about human eating habits. Humans, he says, "don't have claws, and we are not especially fast. We are not like owls, eagles, or raptors, who can recognize a mouse at a hundred yards, swoop down, and capture it. Humans are great apes; our human hands are not designed for ripping apart a fox or a raccoon, but they are really good for picking berries, leaves, and blossoms, just like a chimpanzee would."

Dr. Barnard has applied this assessment of our innate anatomical makeup to his treatment of his patients—and he's done so with great success. "When I take a person who is eating an omnivorous or carnivorous diet and switch them to a plant-based diet," he says, "their arteries open up, they lose weight, and their blood pressure comes down. It's like taking a car that was designed to run on unleaded fuel but for years has been given diesel. The car, which was running ragged, starts to drive properly again. We are not carnivores, have never been carnivores, and a plant-based diet is the best way to go."

Dr. Barnard is not alone in his findings. *The China Study*, a book based on thirty years of research conducted at Cornell and Oxford Universities, examines the idea that degenerative diseases can be prevented on a whole foods, plant-based diet. The popular documentary *Forks Over Knives* traces the journey of *The China Study* author Dr. T. Colin Campbell and another researcher, Dr. Caldwell Esselstyn, both of whom found that "degenerative diseases like heart disease, type 2 diabetes, and even several forms of cancer, could almost always be prevented—and in many cases reversed—by adopting a whole-foods, plant-based diet."[18]

But what about the cultures we have been told thrive on a diet of meat? Researchers studying the Inuit in Alaska have found that they suffer from heart disease and osteoporosis related to a diet high in animal foods. The Maasai in Kenya, who eat a diet high in wild hunted meats, have a life expectancy below fifty years of age.[19] By contrast, the longest living populations consume diets low on animal food. Okinawa, Japan; Sardinia, Italy; Nicoya, Costa Rica; Ikaria, Greece; and Loma Linda, California are all areas called "Blue Zones"—places of the world where there are the highest concentration of people living beyond one hundred years. What is their secret to longevity? Exercise, a sense of purpose, and eating a plant-based diet are among the cornerstone of most of these centenarians' diets.[20] Adopting a plant-based lifestyle is the new taste of nutrition, and it can have a profound impact on health and longevity—yours as well as the planet's.

THE BIGGER PICTURE

*"I've had an epiphany recently . . . I want to challenge all of you as
people of deep conscience, people who are environment stewards of
the earth and oceans . . . By changing what you eat, you will change the
entire contract between the human species and the natural world."*

—James Cameron, filmmaker and Academy Award–winning director

If you doubt that greenhouse gasses are warming the planet, or that
the polar ice caps are melting rapidly, then this section may not be for
you. But if you agree with the overwhelming number of scientists who
are urging us all to address the worsening state of our planet, then you
should realize that consuming a plant-based diet is perhaps the single
most important beneficial act that you can take to reduce your carbon
footprint and fight climate change.

5 WAYS A PLANT-BASED DIET CAN HELP THE PLANET

1. Reduces Global Warming
Droughts, melting polar ice caps, and rising sea levels are consequences
of global warming. Recycling, using energy-efficient lighting, and driving energy-efficient cars can help stem these tides—but a Cornell University study found that producing animal-based protein requires eight
times more energy than producing plant-based protein.

2. Reduces Greenhouse Gases
Cow farts create methane—a gas that both smells bad and is heating up
the planet. According to the United Nations, animal agriculture is a bigger
contributor to greenhouse gas than all forms of transportation.

3. Saves Water
According to John Robbins, author of *The Food Revolution*, producing
one pound of beef requires 1,847 gallons of water, while producing a

pound of broccoli, cauliflower, and Brussels sprouts takes only 34 gallons. "You may save more water by not eating a pound of beef than you would by not showering for six entire months," writes Robbins.

4. Protects the Rainforests
Raising animals for food contributes to deforestation. According to the *World Rainforest Report*, 40 percent of all the rainforests in Central America have been cleared or burned down in the last forty years—mostly for cattle pastures to feed the export market, a large portion of which goes to make US beef burgers.

5. Saves Energy
A publication in the *Journal of Earth Interactions* compared the energy consumption that underlies five popular diets—the Standard American, red meat, fish, poultry, and vegetarian—and the vegetarian diet turned out to be the most energy-efficient of all of these diets.

A whole foods, plant-based diet is good for you, the planet, and (though it may sound a little strange) your canine friends, too. I found this out firsthand with my dog Dakota.

Dakota & Carlyn

In the past I've fed my dogs meat, poultry, and eggs—but as an ethical vegan this decision was always heart-wrenching for me. Looking into the eyes of a chicken, pot-bellied pig, or cow isn't so different for me than looking into the eyes of my own dogs or cats: I see a living, breathing sentient being that feels pain, joy, loss, and love. Each of these animals could easily become a member of our family, so why should one be sacrificed for the other? This is the moral dilemma I was faced with when preparing my dogs' food.

Then I met Jan Alegretti, cowriter of The Complete Holistic Dog Book: Home Health Care for Our Canine Companion, *and her Great Dane, Tila. Tila's coat was black, lustrous and silky to the touch. I wondered what Jan fed her to get these results. I was floored when she told me Tila's* diet was completely plant-based. Another surprising detail: Tila was twelve years old (far older than the average Great Dane's life span, which is six to eight years).

When my dog Dakota started to slow down, the vet told me she had kidney disease that would worsen over time. Dakota was fourteen, had arthritis in her spine, and was panting more and more as she walked. Any pressure to her lower back would make her back legs collapse. Dakota's walks grew shorter as her energy waned. It got to the point where I had to carry her up the stairs, which was taking a toll on my back, too.

I called Jan, hoping she could help—and she did. With her guidance, I put together a variety of plant-based meals for Dakota. Jan taught me that variety is key to the success of this diet; you need to include a mix of vegetables, nuts, seeds, oils, beans, legumes, and grains. So, as I made Dakota's food, I'd think, "Variety, variety, and variety"—and as a result I began adding more "variety, variety, variety" to my own diet. I started adding more purples from cabbage and kale, more red from beets and tomatoes, more greens from chard, broccoli, and peas, more varieties of grains, such as black and brown rice, quinoa, and millet, and more beans and legumes. The better my dog's diet became, the better mine did, too.

I had plenty of doubts about the diet I was offering my beloved dog. Unlike humans, dogs are clearly omnivores: they run after prey, their incisors are long, and their digestive tracts, though not as short as those of felines, can support a more meat-based diet. But seven months later, Dakota's improved health and lab results destroyed all my doubts. In less than a year, she dropped seven pounds and her energy skyrocketed. On our walks, neighbors would comment on her playfulness and renewed spunk. Some even asked how old my new puppy was and were shocked when I would say, "No, this is Dakota!"

Dakota had never been much of a ballplayer, but now she started to insist that we throw her ball so she can chase it. At this point, when I pushed down on her rump, her legs no longer collapsed under my touch. And when her blood tests came back, I was told her kidney levels had also improved.

"Whatever you are doing, keep doing it," my vet told me. And I did.

I know my cats and dogs won't live forever, but I do want them to live as long as they can, with the best quality of life possible. Since our animal *friends' life spans are so much shorter than ours, every extra year, month, or day is precious. Seeing Dakota's transformation, I realized that if a dog, a natural omnivore, can benefit from a plant-based diet, then humans, who are natural herbivores, can thrive on it.*

(Note: Although Dakota's health improved on a plant-based diet, I am not suggesting following this dietary protocol with cats, who are obligate carnivores. There are vegan cat foods on the market that you can check out. Please consult an expert if you are going down that path.)

A DIET OF COMPASSION

We aren't born with a desire to eat animals. As young children, we feel comforted by the teddy bears, pink pigs, and fuzzy lambs on our beds. We are read fairy tales with animals in them, and are taught valuable life lessons through these stories. If we are lucky, our parents relent to our yearning and one day a real live animal companion steps through our front door. The magic of this first love fills our hearts—and it's a magic that may be unmatched for a long time to come.

Studies show that we become more empathetic humans when we learn to be kind to animals.[21] Yet at the same time we are taught that eating them is normal. When babies grow into children, their normal curiosity about the meat on their plates leads to questions: Where does this hamburger come from? Is this from a real chicken like the one on Grandpa's farm? Is this the fish like the one in the tank at our dentist's office? Uncomfortable questions like these are often ignored, or dismissed. And as we grow up, the connection we make between the animals we have loved and the animals on our plates begins to fade as we become absorbed into our "normal, meat-eating culture."

When I left for college, I became a vegetarian. Thirty years later, I became a vegan. In 2011, I was named PETA's "Sexiest Vegetarian Over 50." For the record, I don't really consider myself terribly sexy, but I am very proud of the title because I know the impact that being vegan has upon the world.

In the US, billions of animals are slaughtered for food every year. Being vegan saves nearly two hundred animals per year.[22] This one lifestyle change cannot only add years to *your* life, it can also help the many innocent factory farm animals who endure unimaginable suffering, including branding, dehorning, castration, and death. Remember, factory farms exist because we support them with our dollars. But it doesn't have to be this way. A plant-based diet allows you to take yourself out of this equation by leaving meat off your plate altogether.

If you feel unsure about where to start, take a few moments to determine what motivates you the most about adopting a plant-based diet. Is it your health that you are concerned with? Does the state of the environment that you are leaving behind for your children and grandchildren worry you? Or, like me, is your greatest motivator a desire to lessen the suffering of animals? No matter who you are, if you want to change the world, you can do so, one meal at a time. The choice is ultimately yours.

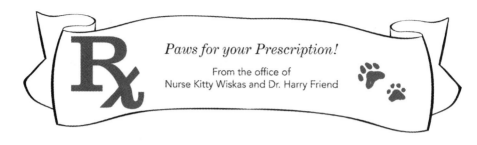

Paws for your Prescription!

From the office of
Nurse Kitty Wiskas and Dr. Harry Friend

1. Going plant-based is a win-win-win! A win for your personal health, a win for our planet, and a win for our farm-animal friends.

2. Are you ready to go plant-based but aren't sure where to start? Check out the wonderful programs brought to you by our awesome friends at Physicians Committee For Responsible Medicine (PCRM.org) or People for the Ethical Treatment of Animals (Prime.Peta.org.) Take a thirty-day challenge or simply start with a Meatless Monday. You don't have to be perfect, just start today.

3. Good food choices are often about common sense. Don't skip over the basics. The magic bullet may not be found in a pill, but it might just begin with an apple a day!

COMING UP: Did you and your animal friends enjoy a healthy breakfast this morning? Are you ready to energize your well-being? Then let's get moving!

CHAPTER 4

Fitness With Friends

"If your dog is fat, you aren't getting enough exercise."

—Anonymous

We may kick, scream, and complain about doing it, but we all know that in order to have a healthy life now and in our later years, we need to regularly engage in some form of physical exercise. Whether you are a child, adult, bona fide couch potato, or just someone who struggles with inertia from time to time, moving is great medicine—and it will stack the odds of well-being in your favor.

Studies show us that exercising, even if for just thirty minutes a day, decreases a person's risk of diabetes and high blood pressure and positively affects their mood.[23] Sitting for three hours a day or more, in contrast, has been shown to decrease our life span by promoting chronic disease, even if you exercise regularly.[24] If longevity is important to you—and I've found it is to most people—exercise is the key. Blue Zones, the geographic areas of the world where people live longest, show us that one of the secrets to these people's longevity is to exercise, though not at the gym. These centenarians engage, rather, in natural movement activities such as gardening and walking.

Yes, you can go to a gym, put on an exercise DVD, or choose from a myriad of solo exercise routines, but having an exercise buddy, especially a dog, increases your chances of actually putting on your sneakers, walking out of the house, and producing a little sweat.[25] Knowing that your dog depends on you can help you cancel out your excuses, get you more motivated, and encourage you stick to your plans. Plus, what better exercise buddy than one who is enthusiastic about getting outside and who makes the endeavor so much more fun!

Take a look and you will see animal lovers and their exercise buddies everywhere—jogging, hiking, playing Frisbee, and even bike riding. Why not join them? If you've been sitting at your computer for a while and your dog nudges your knee with her nose or your cat jumps on your keyboard, don't get mad and brush them away. Instead, why not heed your best friend's advice and get up out of your chair. These are the moments when your cat and dog, in their own unique way, may just be saving your life.

WALKING TOWARDS WELLNESS

"A journey of a thousand miles begins with a single step."

—Lao Tzu

Thirty minutes of brisk walking is what the surgeon general recommends as a daily minimum for every American to shape up.[26] Luckily, this is a piece of the fitness puzzle where your dog can really help you out.

"The Walk" is an ancient exercise that serves us well in these modern times, especially for those of us who are dog lovers seeking a greater connection with our canine companions. My four dogs have been my constant, committed, and reliable walking partners over the years, and I can honestly say that if it weren't for them, I would spend a lot more time on the couch. And fitness is just one of the benefits of this wonderful practice.

5 BENEFITS OF WALKING YOUR DOG

1. It's a powerful mood booster (and since we know that dogs can make us feel happier anyway, walking your dog can act like a double dose of happy juice).
2. The 34 percent of dog guardians who walk their dogs regularly are more likely than others to be physically fit.[27]
3. People who don't have dogs tend to talk themselves out of exercising more often than those that have a dog companion.[28]
4. Walking is great for your heart. Dogs are great for your heart. Need I say more?
5. Walking your canine friend builds a connection with your dog, and with others, too! Dog lovers will often strike up conversations and become friends with other dog lovers.[29]

A backyard is great if you have a dog but it can never take the place of walking them. Imagine that for the rest of your life you could never go any farther than your house and yard. Wouldn't you eventually grow bored? It's the same for dogs; they might enjoy sunbathing, digging holes, or playing in their yards, but none of that will ever come close to the physical and mental stimulation that a walk with their favorite human provides.

Walking your dog also offers you the chance to absorb some vitamin D from the sun, according to researcher Dr. Michael Holick, author of *The Vitamin D Solution*. As many as 75 percent of Americans are at risk of vitamin D deficiency, due in large part to their failure to get enough sunshine.[30] Optimizing your vitamin D levels contributes to a healthy heart, your body's ability to fight infection, and is important for cancer prevention. So get outside—and bring your dog with you!

SENSES & SENSIBILITY

Humans usually take walks to get some exercise, but dogs love to go for the *experience of walking*. For a dog, walking is a powerful sensory adventure.

The journey is about what they smell, hear, taste, feel, and see. And that is something we humans can learn from them when we walk together.

When was the last time you savored your food rather than gobbled it down? Or took a moment to feel the warmth of the hand that just shook yours? Have you ever noticed the distinct voices of the many birds chirping outside your window? Do you notice the scents that arrive with the changing seasons? How often have you passed a tree and stopped to watch the sun's rays penetrating through its branches?

Through their senses, dogs see a world that we humans often take for granted. Watching our dogs explore their environments with wonder and excitement can be a great reminder for us to tune into *right now* instead of thinking about past memories or worrying about future events that haven't yet occurred.

Most cats may not be able to go on long hikes or catch a Frisbee in midair, but because they have keen senses (often superior even to those of our canine buddies), we can learn a thing or two about staying present even when they are not with us. Did you know, for example, that cats see things panoramically when they dilate their pupils? Humans, meanwhile, tend to do the opposite—we focus in on a very narrow field of vision—and often suffer from super-myopia as a result. Okay, I made up the term "super-myopia," but doesn't the concept fit? Myopia is "tunnel vision," and we humans fall prey to this narrow way of looking at the world when our minds are wrapped up in our thoughts, concerns, and worries—which is most of the time.

Take thirty seconds to hear like your cat and you may be surprised to find nature speaking through the rustling trees, a child's laughter, or crashing waves. You may not be able to pick up the distant scents your cat does, but you may just be able to smell the lavender or the wild peppermint on the side of the road. We can't solve all of our problems by drinking in the exquisite colors of a sunset or feeling an ocean breeze on our face, but these fleeting moments can nurture us in ways that nothing else can. Just ask Michelle, whose cat brings her closer to nature, comforts her, and has given her hope at a time when she has needed it the most.

Abbey, Alley, Mike & Michelle

When we first got married, my husband and I used to take long walks together along the beach in Carpinteria, a small coastal town in southern California. Mike and I loved our time together outdoors, and being so close to nature made us feel lucky.

Mike has Parkinson's disease, and when the disease took a turn for the worse, our lives changed forever. Although Mike pushed bravely forward and tried to maintain his daily activities, he grew more and more physically unstable. Eventually, we came to the realization that we could no longer go out on walks together. This was heartbreaking for both of us.

We moved from the sunny beaches of southern California to Sonoma, four hundred miles north, so Mike could be closer to his family. My daily walks continued, but as I headed out my front door, I felt sad leaving Mike behind.

One day, I had walked about half a block when out of nowhere I heard a cat chattering up a storm. I turned to find Abbey—our sweet calico cat—trailing along behind me.

We had adopted Abbey from the Humane Society as a kitten. The moment Mike laid eyes on her, he fell in love. There was an indescribable bond between them. We took Abbey home that day, and then, two days later, we went back and got Abbey's sister, Alley.

It had been two years since Mike had stopped walking with me, and now here was Abbey, racing to catch up to me. At first I worried about her darting in front of a car or chasing a lizard, but Abbey stayed right by my side for the entire walk. The next day, she followed me again, and the next day yet again. She has now been my walking partner on this special morning ritual for the last three years. Together we walk under the ornamental pear trees that turn white in the spring. When the winds blow, it looks like you are walking through falling snow. Abbey loves to play with the white leaves as they float to the ground. It's a beautiful sight.

One of the hardest things in the world is to watch helplessly as someone you love suffers from an incurable disease. Mike was once an excellent tennis player and had dreams of traveling the world, but at forty-nine he had to give up those dreams. Somehow, both Abbey and Alley seem to know *what Mike needs and when he needs it. At times they snuggle against his legs, purring and kneading him and their touch comforts him. But at other times, when his body becomes rigid, Mike says it feels like his legs are made of cement, and he can't tolerate touch. At these times the cats give Mike his space. They also seem to know when to provide a much-needed laugh, and that's when they will leap into the air or do something funny.*

Being Mike's primary caretaker has taken a toll on me. The work is hard, and I run through a gamut of emotions every week, from anger to depression. Abbey and Alley seem to sense my grief. Sometimes they sit and stare at me as if thinking, Hmmm, how can I help?

Some days I don't feel like going out, but now that Abbey is my walking buddy I have no choice. Once 10 A.M. strikes, Abbey lets me know it's time to go. She gets my attention by bumping my ankles with her head—and if that doesn't work, she meows and puckers her mouth, making a funny face that makes me laugh. If I still am not out the door after all that, she jumps on the kitchen counter and begins to slide things off of it with her paw. The other day she picked up my necklace and ran down the hallway until I caught her.

Abbey's companionship on my daily walks has not only eased my loneliness, it has brought me closer to my neighbors. They are amazed at how she stays so close to me without a leash, which has sparked many conversations. And Abbey even joins my ninety-five-year-old neighbor Cecilia on her rounds delivering our community newsletter.

Because Abbey has touched the lives of so many people, we have made many new friends, and we get invited to a lot more gatherings. For both Mike and me, it is important that people see him for who he is, not just "the guy with Parkinson's who uses a walker." Because of Abbey and Alley, we hope they now see us as the nice couple with the great cats.

I grieve for what my husband once was, and I grieve for what will never be. But life feels "normal" when Mike laughs at Abbey and Alley chasing each other through the house on a rainy day. I would be on Prozac if it were not for those two. There is no better therapy in the world than a cat as a companion. Abbey and Alley are a needed reminder that life is good, and that there is hope.

THE YIN & THE YANG OF IT

According to Chinese medicine, in order to enjoy vibrant health, we need to live in balance with nature. Ill health results from an imbalance of two forces: yin and yang. Everything in the natural world is made of yin and yang—day and night, summer and winter, fire and water. These forces are opposite yet complementary because neither can ultimately survive without the other, and the balance of these energies creates well-being.

Because dogs are generally more playful and active, I associate them with the masculine, yang type of energy. Cats, on the other hand, with their quiet, more feminine, and nocturnal ways, are more yin. The qualities of yin in our cats and yang in our dogs can serve to remind us of the necessity of balance when it comes to our exercise choices.

Although walking is an excellent opportunity for humans to get the exercise they need, and very necessary for dogs, too, it shouldn't be our only activity. It's extremely important for us to add some stretching to keep us flexible and limber, like our cat friends model for us. If you are a cat lover, you know how intoxicating it is to watch our cats stretch their bodies until they give that little shiver at the end when they have reached their limit.

Over time, our human bodies give in to gravity—our shoulders begin to stoop, we get injured more easily, and we wake up more often with aches and pains. I cannot say enough about yoga and tai chi as counterbalances to gravity's effects, and for longevity. Animals have influenced both of these Eastern practices. The early yogis and tai chi masters would watch animals in nature and mimic them to embrace their energies and wisdom. There's a reason you see so many people today engaging in these yin-type practices, especially as they age; they help us to manage our stress, stay in shape, and keep vital.

We all need yin and yang in our lives. Walking our dogs is great for activating the yang energy within us; mirroring our cats' stretching is the perfect way to nurture our yin. Together, these exercises serve to remind us that optimal well-being is about balance and harmony with the natural world around us.

THE UGLIEST DOG I HAVE EVER SEEN

In 2001 I was working seventy hours a week on a TV show and studying several hours a day for my acupuncture exams. In my "spare time," I married the love of my life, Ken, and became a stepmom to Greg and Gina. In the middle of all this chaos and change, Roxy came to live with us.

I was driving to Hollywood one day when a German shepherd ran out into traffic. After pulling over and somehow luring her into my backseat, I decided the most pragmatic thing to do would be to bring her to the closest shelter. I didn't feel good about leaving her there, but I lived twenty-five miles away, and I figured that if her guardians were looking for her, they would look for her there. I left a deposit ensuring that if no one came for her they would relinquish her to my care.

I visited the dog regularly over the ensuing weeks and on one of my visits I found she had a new roommate: a smaller shepherd who was whining and pacing, clearly upset by her stressful surroundings. To this day, I don't know why I didn't see the sign with the large letters warning me to keep my hands out of the cage, but I didn't. So my hand went straight through the chain link, trying to coax the dog I was there to visit toward me. She didn't budge, but the smaller shepherd lay down in front of me and gently laid her paw on top of my hand. Then her chin came down and rested on top of both. Her anxiety diminished in one long, deep sigh.

I don't know how much time passed, but during those seconds I stopped hearing the cacophony of dog howling and barks or any other sounds. Though I was certain the world was still spinning, it felt as if nothing else existed except for this four-legged being and me. In the silence, a knowing transpired; I knew that this little shepherd was meant for me—and I for her.

I called my husband and began telling him the story, but I only got as far as "and then she put her paw on my hand" before he stopped me and said, "Bring her home, bring them both home."

The larger shepherd never came home with us. Her guardians came for her soon after. But when Roxy arrived at our house, Ken took one look at her and said matter-of-factly, "I think this may be the ugliest dog I have ever seen."

He didn't say this to be mean; he said it because Roxy had been through the mill and she looked it. No matter how many times I bathed her she still looked haggard and smelled like rotten fish.

But her physical issues were not the only problem; Roxy brought several pieces of baggage with her: aggression towards people, other dogs, and even cats.

I had grown up with dogs my whole life, but I'd never had one like this. Even after I trained her, Roxy had more issues than I knew how to deal with. I needed help—and fortunately, I got it.

Roxy, Cesar & Carlyn

Six months after I brought Roxy home, I opened the Los Angeles Times and saw a picture that has forever stuck in my mind: a muscular thirty-something-year-old man was walking through a canyon flanked by Rottweilers, pit bulls, and other assorted street dogs; in his backpack, he carried a Chihuahua. The man was Cesar Millan, known by millions as "The Dog Whisperer," and the article said that his specialty was working with aggressive dogs through dog psychology.

It had taken me several months to admit to myself that I actually even had an aggressive dog. I played the denial game—"Roxy's really not that bad"—even after she bit my brother's arm as he pulled a beer out of a cooler. Or, "Roxy's just new, I'm sure she'll get over it" after she bit a trainer's shoe . . . while it was still on her foot. And, "Oh look, she just wants to play" as she wagged her tail at another dog . . . just before lunging at them.

When Roxy nipped a neighbor's child, I finally picked up the phone and discovered that Cesar was giving a workshop near Templeton, California. Immediately, I signed us up.

When we arrived at the horse ranch where the workshop was being held, Roxy began to yip, growl, and lunge at the other dogs in attendance. To keep the peace, I walked her to the far corner of the arena until Cesar made his entrance.

"Who has the most aggressive dog here?" he asked right when he walked in.

I looked around to see who that would be, then realized that everyone was pointing at me.

Roxy wasn't born aggressive; human cruelty and neglect had turned a loving, smart, and vibrant dog into an anxious and aggressive one. (After adopting her, I learned that police had brought her to the shelter after a drug arrest in Watts.) Although I was protective of Roxy, I felt I could trust this man, so I handed her leash to him.

"Two more aggressive dogs," he said to the group. A Great Dane and a golden retriever were handed to him. With the two dogs' leashes in one hand and Roxy's in the other, Cesar began walking away from us and around the horse arena. Realizing she was moving away from me, Roxy's barking and whining escalated, but Cesar just kept walking as if nothing unusual was taking place. He passed behind a large tree, and a moment later, when he came out the other side, all three dogs were walking quietly and in unison. The change was so immediate and unexpected that the group gave one loud, collective gasp. I could feel my eyes welling up. It was as if I had a child that no one else had ever been willing to play with, and for the first time she was fitting in. It was an incredible feeling, as though anything was possible in the world.

Cesar came over to where I was standing, handed me all three leashes, and said, "Now it's your turn."

I took the leashes with a false sense of confidence and began to walk.

"Wait, wait, wait a minute. Why are you so tense?" I heard Cesar say behind me.

"Because I know what she's capable of," I responded without reservation.

"That was yesterday, Carlyn. Today is a new day."

For the next several hours I learned two things that forever changed my relationship not only with Roxy but with all dogs:

1. Dogs, especially those with emotional imbalances, thrive on walking as a way to help release pent-up energy.

2. Your dog's leash can act as a conductor, and the type of energy you carry can travel down that leash and affect your dog's behavior as you walk them. Dogs sense energy; if you walk with stress, anger, or frustration, they feel those emotions and can respond with raised hackles at an approaching dog or human, or even a squirrel. Conversely, if you walk out in the world with a more positive, confident disposition, your dog will feel that energy instead. Their behavior may not change overnight, but they can shift little by little over time, just like humans do.

The more I worked with Roxy from this mindset, the better she became, and in time she could walk past other dogs, humans, or children without feeling threatened. Years later, when I told people about Roxy's early aggressive behavior, they would look at her face sweetly staring up at them, then look at me as if I were the world's biggest fibber and say, "This dog? No way!"

That day with Cesar was the first time I was formally introduced to the energy that exists between humans and animals. Since then, I have spent thousands of hours walking with my dogs and using their behavior as a barometer for my mental state. It's curious how they will often misbehave when I'm not feeling at my emotional best. If I'm moody, overwhelmed, or tense from stress, they act up and reflect that right back to me.

I thought I was training Roxy by using a leash. I didn't realize that my own transformation awaited me on the other side of it.

Paws for your Prescription!

From the office of
Nurse Kitty Wiskas and Dr. Harry Friend

1. We dogs make great walking buddies. Make sure you walk with us every day . . . twice!

2. Arching, bending, and stretching are a cat's forte. When you see us do this, take a few minutes to try it with us.

3. Before you exercise with us, consider our needs. Pugs may not be the best dogs to take jogging, Australian shepherds will need more activity than a leisurely stroll, and we cats . . . well, we generally prefer to lie on your back while you do yoga. Make the experience mutually gratifying: good for you, and good for us.

COMING UP: You and your dog are now enjoying your daily walks. And although you are feeling more energized, your cat's alluring purr is making you become very, very, sleepy . . .

CHAPTER 5

The Sick and the Sleepless

"Why do cats sleep so much? Perhaps they've been trusted with some major cosmic task, an essential law of physics—such as: if there are less than 5 million cats sleeping at any one time the world will stop spinning. So that when you look at them and think, 'What a lazy, good-for-nothing animal,' they are, in fact, working very, very hard."

—Kate Atkinson

Several years ago, I went through one of the most painful periods of my life. Leaving a marriage can feel devastating, even under the best of circumstances. And although the decision to divorce was mutually reached by both my husband and myself, my heart still felt broken, my self-esteem nose-dived, and my ability to sleep vanished.

Until this point, I had always slept like a baby. But now I would lay awake late into the night, watching reruns on TV or surfing the Internet. Perhaps it was because a bed once shared now felt too lonely, or maybe it's that it hurt too much to be alone with my thoughts—either way, sleep eluded me, often until the early hours.

To compound my problem, I began to have a nightly affair . . . with Ben and Jerry. Dipping into a quart of coffee ice cream had a way of putting a smile back on my face. But the smile faded after a routine doctor's visit when lab tests came back revealing high blood sugar levels. To add insult to injury, the doctor's scale showed an extra fifteen pounds. That was the moment I finally decided to grab the rudder of my flailing ship and steer myself toward healthier shores.

INSOMNIAC NATION

My story is personal, but it is not unique. Up to 70 million Americans suffer from chronic sleep problems, according to the Centers for Disease Control and Prevention (CDC).[31] Chronic sleep deprivation, which is defined as regularly getting less than six hours of sleep per night, has been linked to many health issues, including neurological problems, diabetes, anxiety, obesity, and even cancer. Sleep deprivation interferes with our work, our social activities, and our relationships. If you are one of the millions who suffer from sleep problems, you probably understand better than anyone why lack of sleep is so effective as a means of torture.

Sleep deprivation can affect anyone, but some of the hardest hit are shift workers, medical interns, and first-year college students. And when people drive after being awake for seventeen to nineteen hours, studies show they perform worse than those who have a blood alcohol level of .05 percent.[32]

If you feel that you are A-okay on just six hours of sleep or less each night, here's some food for thought: researchers at the University of Pennsylvania's Perelman School of Medicine discovered that prolonged periods without sleep led to diminished neural function and loss of brain cells—damage that they think may be irreversible.[33]

Still not convinced that you should get to bed earlier? Not getting enough shut-eye may actually be the reason you're thinking this way. Lack of sleep impairs our judgment, *especially about how much sleep we need.* "Studies show that over time, people who are getting six hours of sleep, instead of seven or eight, begin to feel that they've adapted to that sleep deprivation," says sleep expert Phil Gehrman, PhD. "But if you look at how they actually do on tests of mental alertness and performance, they continue to go downhill. So there's a point in sleep deprivation when we lose touch with how impaired we are."[34]

The short of it is, if you are sleeping less than seven hours a night, you probably aren't sleeping enough—even if you think you are.

THE COST OF THE ETERNAL DAY

Edison's light bulb has given us the opportunity to do more, play more, and create more into the night hours—but that advantage has come with a price tag, not only for humans but for other species as well.

Birds use the moon and the stars to help them navigate during their migrations and flying over brightly lit areas can leave them disoriented. In fact, Michael Mesure, executive director of the Fatal Light Awareness Program, reported to *National Geographic* that entire flocks of bird species who migrate across North America sometimes collide. He cited as an example the *50,000* birds that died when they followed lights straight into the ground over an Air Force base in Georgia.[35]

Newly hatched sea turtles can mistake artificial light for moonlight, causing them to wander inland where they die of dehydration instead of out to sea.[36] And artificial lighting has also adversely affected the DNA, mating activities, and physical development of frogs.[37]

Although few studies have yet to be done on mammals like our cat and dog friends, would it really surprise you if artificial lights did not have a negative effect on them, considering it has a detrimental effect on the closest mammal you know—you?

Both Chinese and Western medicine show a correlation between lack of sleep and heart health. Western medical studies show us that heart disease, heart attacks, and high blood pressure can be linked to chronic sleep deprivation. In Chinese medicine, we believe that when you fall asleep at night, the *shen*—your spirit—finds rest in the heart. But if you are still awake, the shen cannot rest. Over time, "disturbed shen" can lead to anxiety, depression, and even psychosis.

Basically, poor sleeping habits make very poor bedfellows.

YOU ARE NOW GETTING VERY, VERY SLEEPY . . .

I'm not trying to hypnotize you. Actually, maybe I am. I would love for everyone reading this to put a good night's sleep at the top of his or her priority list. Here are some benefits that forty winks can provide . . .

THE BEAUTY IN BEAUTY SLEEP

- Increased vitality
- Decreased stress and more positive mood
- Better focus, attention, and concentration
- Improved memory
- Better metabolism
- Younger-looking skin
- *And much, much more!*

Our cats and dogs are masters of sleep. Dogs sleep nearly half of their lives, twelve to eighteen hours per day. Cats spend about two-thirds of their life, or sixteen to twenty hours daily, sleeping. Unlike their human friends, animals do what comes naturally: they follow their natural sleep cycles. I'm not saying humans should get twelve to twenty hours of sleep per day—I'm just advocating for seven to nine hours of delicious shut-eye.

Below are five ways that you can copycat your four-legged friends as they model what good sleeping habits look like.

1. The Good Night

Staying up to watch movies is my Achilles heel. As a former film editor, I watch movies both for enjoyment and for the craft. But as an acupuncturist, I know staying up late is not the best idea for my overall well-being.

Late one night, after doing some research for this chapter, I plopped myself onto the couch to watch the TV show *Breaking Bad*. Somewhere late into the night, my eyes momentarily unglued themselves from the screen, and I found myself looking around the room at my animal six-pack, the members of which were scattered across the floor, lying on dog beds, and snoozing on the couch. Teddy's snores whistled, Dakota's eyes fluttered. Roxy signature sigh periodically interrupted her breathing, and Rudy's yip-yips and twitching body were sure signs that he was off in dreamland, running with me up a trail. And the cats were down for the count as well: Jester was perched on my legs and Cody was sprawled across my lap. All my animal friends were where they should be at midnight: blissfully asleep. The only animal in the room that *wasn't* asleep was the animal that is supposed to be (according to us, anyway) the smartest on the food chain: me.

Although I had lived through this scene thousands of nights before, tonight was the night that I had my *aha!* I realized that not only was I cheating myself out of a full tank of energy for the following day, I might also be having an adverse effect on the animals that I love with my night-for-day habit. I thought about the birds dying of exhaustion, the turtle hatchlings that never made it to sea, and the frogs that could no longer mate—all because of artificial lighting at night. I thought about how I was going to pay a price for staying up late with a fuzzy head and a cranky attitude the next morning. And I thought about how my animals might also pay a price over time. They depend on me for their well-being, after all, and that means my decisions affect them.

Awareness is an important first step towards lasting change. When I realized *Breaking Bad* could wait but my sleep could not, I turned off the set and got my six-pack and myself to bed. I was grateful to fall asleep to the symphony of frogs outside my window, their voices reminding me that their rhythms and mine aren't so very different.

2. Daytime Siestas Instead of Evening Fiestas

As a child, my mother insisted I take a nap every afternoon. Later, as a college student studying in Madrid, I napped alongside the entire country of Spain. Every day after lunch, the banks, schools, and stores would close their doors and go to sleep. Madrid turned into a ghost city until about 5 P.M., when she would come alive again.

Besides Spain, the afternoon nap is also practiced in Latin America, Greece, and the Philippines. In China and Taiwan it is called the *wujiao*, and in Bangladesh it is known as "rice sleep." In the US the midday rest has another name: the Power Nap.

Some of history's greatest minds—including Albert Einstein, Eleanor Roosevelt, and Thomas Edison—have been nappers. Even the personal physician to the Dalai Lama takes a nap every afternoon at 1 P.M.

If you work long hours or need several cups of coffee or caffeinated sodas to keep awake, try napping. Naps may not completely make up for poor nighttime sleep, but a short nap can improve your mood, increase your alertness, and give your creativity a boost.

They say the Universe brings the teacher when the student is ready. I didn't know my teacher would have green eyes and long whiskers. After my divorce, I suffered from insomnia, which caused me to nod off at work most afternoons. Though I would try to steal a nap, my racing mind and heartache made sleep impossible. One day as I lay on the office couch, Jester jumped onto my back. His warm, soft body and soothing purr worked like magic, and I fell asleep in moments.

These little "cat naps" were like water from a spring. They were saving my life. And they became a regular ritual Monday through Friday until we found Jester his new home: my apartment, where we could continue our siestas on Saturday and Sunday, too.

3. ExerciZZZ

Remember the Surgeon General's recommendation of thirty minutes of exercise for daily health? A little exercise can also lead you towards a glorious, rejuvenating, and life-enhancing night of sleep.

Whether it is walking, bicycling or swimming, your favorite exercise done thirty to forty minutes four times a week can improve your sleep quality. If you are out walking your dog and you catch some sunlight on the way, even better: this allows your body to boost its levels of serotonin, a hormone and neurotransmitter that is associated with optimal sleep.

And let's not forget our feline friends. Who better than our beloved cats to model the grace of stretching with their enviable bending and impressive arching? In humans, stretching can increase circulation and promote relaxation. In a study done at Fred Hutchinson Cancer Research Center in Seattle, women who stretched four times a week for fifteen to thirty minutes reduced their difficulty with falling asleep by 30 percent.[38] Yoga, the five-thousand-year-old art of stretching, has been shown to help relax our nervous systems, which are often on overdrive from our busy lives.[39] When doing yoga at home before bedtime, I have often relaxed to the point of falling asleep while still in a pose . . . and woken up to find a tuxedo cat purring on my back.

4. The Nightly Ritual

According to a recent survey by the American Pet Products Association, nearly half of dogs and 75 percent of cats sleep with their guardians. If you're allergic to animals or are easily disturbed by movement, you may want to keep your dogs or cats in their own beds for the time being. But if you are one of the lucky ones that don't suffer from these problems, then I can't think of anything sweeter and more comforting than sharing your bed with your animal friends.

According to the ASPCA, dogs are happier sleeping with other dogs or cats, or in a room with a human family member.[40] In my home my bed isn't quite as big as my heart, so it's just me, Ken, and the cats who sleep on the bed, while Roxy, Dakota, Teddy, and Rudy sleep on cushy beds on the floor around us.

If you have sleep issues, take some quality time with your cat or dog before bedtime. These moments spent together bonding in your favorite ways can help you wind down and relieve stress. Some of my favorite pre-sleep activities are to gently massage my dogs' backs, stroke their ears, or brush their fur. With my cats, I also may brush them with a cat comb, or just lie beside them and listen to them purr. Sometimes, this proves so soothing that I find myself drifting off while still on a dog bed, until a paw nudges me awake and reminds of my purpose . . . to serve, not sleep.

5. Dreamscapes with Four Legs

Dreams are a mystery. We know very little about why we dream or how dreams work. But we do know that our dreams are important for processing our emotions and stress. Studies have also shown that they are vital for learning and developing new skills.[41]

As your bond with your animal companion grows, you may start to see cats and dogs popping up in your dreamscapes. Pay attention to these symbols; exploring the meanings behind them may help you understand something deeper about yourself.

Although I have found no scientific evidence to support dream interpretation, the ancient civilizations of Mesopotamia and Rome regarded the art as invaluable. In Egypt and Greece, dreams were considered to be messages sent from the gods. And Hippocrates, the father of Western medicine, would ask his patients about their dreams to gather clues as to what might be affecting them physically.

If a cat or dog shows up in your dreams, they may represent an important message that shouldn't be missed. Recording your dreams in a journal will help you remember the messages the gods—or your furry friends—may be trying to share with you, and may help you get to the "aha" of a problem or reveal a nugget of wisdom.

Making sense of our dreams and their hidden messages can be therapeutic. By paying attention to the animals in our dream life, we can make better sense of our days, our challenges, and ultimately our lives.

Paws for your Prescription!

From the office of
Nurse Kitty Wiskas and Dr. Harry Friend

1. Make sleep a priority for you, *and for us.* Start tonight!

2. Mirror our amazing sleeping techniques, such as upside down and belly up!

3. Take a cat nap during the day for a purrfect boost of energy.

4. Enjoy a daily walk or two with your favorite canine and we will all sleep better at night.

COMING UP: You are becoming the master of your day! You have begun a morning ritual, and your Meatless Monday has turned into a Tofu Tuesday. You're walking twice a day and tonight you have committed to switching your lights off by 10 P.M. How many more ways can your animal friends help you to be physically healthier? Read on and find out!

CHAPTER 6

Super Kids

"The best doctor in the world is a wet nose and a wagging tail."

—Jill Robinson

In the US, 40 percent of our animal friends live in families with children under eighteen years of age. Open any kid's book or watch any popular children's movie, and chances are you'll find cats and dogs making an appearance. The reason is clear: our four-legged friends are virtually guaranteed to put a smile on a child's face when they see them. That must be why the words "dog," "cat," "woof-woof" and "kitty" are some of the most frequently occurring words in a young child's vocabulary.[42]

Animals and kids connect, heart to heart, soul to soul—perhaps because they are so very similar. Both animals and children seem to be in touch with an innocence that fades as we grow older and move into our later acts of life.

According to the theory of biophilia (introduced and popularized by Harvard professor Edward O. Wilson in the 1980s), there is an instinctive bond between humans and the natural world—including animals.[43] This bond, Wilson says, is rooted in our biology. In other words, we may be a hardwired to love animals from birth.

The future of our world depends on our children growing into healthy, happy, and extraordinary adults. Yet we are living in a time when that goal may feel more challenging than ever. Today, a child's world can be unsettling on a personal level (for example, in the case of divorce, death, and other household disruptions), and also on a global level as the health of our environment becomes more precarious. More than ever before in history, our children are experiencing a growing isolation as technology decreases our connection to nature and increases our attachment to gadgets.

Advances in medicine are supposed to help us to live longer. But parents of today's children may end up outliving their offspring. Diabetes and obesity, conditions previously reserved for adults, are now becoming more common in childhood.[44] And physical diseases aren't the only health challenges affecting children: teen suicide rates have tripled as anxiety and depression have also risen. ADHD, one of the most common neurobehavioral disorders affecting school-age children, is leaving more and more kids with difficulty concentrating. Autism, which leads to trouble communicating, forming relationships, and developing empathy, is also on the rise; it currently affects one in sixty-eight children in the US, an increase of 123 percent between 2002 and 2010.[45]

No one can take the place of a loving, caring, and nurturing parent—but cats and dogs *are* wonderful at riding shotgun and enhancing our efforts. When a child is exposed to an animal early in life, both physical and emotional advantages result. Studies show that if a cat or dog is introduced into a home in their first year, that child will have a lower risk of developing allergies and asthma.[46] Additionally, children with pets in the household are 44 percent less likely to develop ear infections, and 29 percent less likely to receive antibiotics in their first year; living with a furry friend gives children's immune systems a great boost for life.[47]

Today, one in three children in the US are considered overweight or obese.[48] Besides the potential for serious health problems down the road, the extra weight can bring on criticism from classmates and peers—no surprise, as our media tells us all too frequently that to be beautiful means to be skinny. Having a cat or dog companion who loves their child unconditionally, whatever size the child may be, is a boon to a little one's self worth. And a four-legged family member can provide a calming presence, a feeling of safety, and a decrease in stress levels for any child.[49]

Another kid-related bonus to having a dog: Because our best friends need to be walked daily, dogs are great motivators to get kids moving. A study conducted in England found that kids with dogs were less likely to be overweight or obese.[50] Walking, running, and playing fetch with a dog can encourage a child to be more active, makes exercise fun, and helps them develop good habits into adulthood.

Children with ADHD can also benefit from having an animal companion in the home. Having a cat or dog to look after can be a great way for a child who exhibits hyperactive behavior to learn responsibility and focus. Playing with or walking a dog is an excellent means of releasing the pent-up energy a child with ADHD accumulates. Having another being who loves them unconditionally, isn't judging them, and helps keep them calm is priceless for these children.

Similarly to what they offer kids with ADHD, a feline or canine friend can be a calming influence on autistic children—one that also teaches them about empathy. "It's a very positive experience for a child or adolescent to take on the responsibility of caring for a cat or a dog because the immediate feedback is an animal's gratitude and affection," says Donald Sherak, a psychiatrist I interviewed who works with autistic children and adolescents in the Boston area. "Animals are touch creatures, and they like physical contact. They like to make their presence known by nuzzling, nudging, and seeking to be petted. When they like a person they do that behavior even more, and kids find that very rewarding."

Do you remember the last time your child felt upset, anxious, or fearful? Did they turn to their cat or dog for support? If so, they're not alone. A study in the UK found that children ranked their relationships with their animals sometimes higher than certain human relationships. And 75 percent of the participating children said they sought out their companions when they were upset.[51] It appears that in some cases, animals are the *only* friends some children have. Animals don't criticize or show their disapproval like a human might, so it stands to reason that a child would feel safe in their presence.

When I spoke to Pamela J. Kimmel, a marriage and family therapist who works with emotionally challenged children, about the connection between children and animals, she shared this touching story with me:

Last spring I was with one of my clients, a nine-year-old boy, at a playground adjacent to the school. The little boy was extremely angry and aggressive, so being outside and doing something physical was a great way for him to relax and stay focused. While we were at the playground a young man with two pit bull puppies walked up to us. The puppies were friendly, and much to my surprise and amusement, they ran over to the slide, climbed up the ladder, and slid down. The puppies kept doing this over and over for several minutes. While this was going on I observed the look on my client's face. I knew he was relating to these puppies because his expression changed from anger and sadness to one of joy. I had never seen him laugh or smile before. It was such a beautiful moment, and it will stay with me forever."

DOCTOR DOG

While researching this book, I had the pleasure of speaking with Jill Robinson. Jill is a tireless animal advocate and founder of The Animals Asia Foundation, an organization devoted to improving the welfare of animals throughout China and Vietnam. Jill, a soft-spoken English woman, shared with me a moment of inspiration that she had with her dog, Max. That moment started something that has touched the lives of countless sick children *and* their dog doctors.

Max & Jill

When I was living in Hong Kong in 1991, there were two issues that troubled me deeply: the abandonment of dogs who were no longer wanted, and the consumption of cats and dogs for the food industry. I very much wanted people to look upon and embrace dogs with greater compassion and respect. And one day, I figured out how.

As I sat reading an article on "pets as therapy," a light bulb went off in my head. I turned to my own dog, a beautiful golden retriever and said, "I think you can do this, Max!"

For the next few weeks, I phoned hospitals, therapy centers, and rest homes, asking if I could bring Max to visit their patients and residents.

But instead of excitement or at least some curiosity on their part, I kept getting the same response: "You're not suggesting bringing a dirty, smelly mutt into our hospital, are you?"

"Well, yes," I would say. The conversations usually ended with a hang-up. But one day, someone finally got curious. The matron at the Duchess of Kent Hospital had heard about pet therapy and agreed to give Max and me a shot at it.

"You have one hour in the garden with one dog," the matron told me.

When the day came, I brought Max to the hospital. For about an hour, we sat in the garden waiting. Finally, a staff member wheeled out a hospital bed where a paraplegic boy lay. Without hesitating, Max walked up to the boy and put his lovely golden paws on his bed. Immediately, the boy's face lit up!

I had invited the media, and now their cameras were clicking repeatedly and flashes were going off everywhere. The hospital staff was incredulous because the boy, who had been sad just a few minutes before, was now so happy. Then the other sick kids joined in on the fun and began bandaging Max's arms just like their arms were bandaged. The children were all clearly having a great time.

The next day, the story was in the newspapers, and our phone started ringing off the hook with calls from hospitals wanting volunteers to bring their dogs to their facilities. This is how the Dr. Dog Program was born. Today we are in seven countries in Asia, with nearly 1,000 dogs in the program.

FOUR-LEGGED TEACHERS

If giving your son's immune system a boost, relieving your daughter's stress, and getting both to exercise aren't enough, consider this: your cat and dog can also help your child improve their reading skills. This was discovered by researchers from UC Davis Veterinary Medicine Extension, and Tony La Russa's Animal Rescue Foundation, who teamed up to study third graders as they read aloud to dogs from the All Ears Reading Program.[52] At the end of ten weeks, the students had improved their reading fluency by 12 percent, while the control group (who read without dogs) did not improve at all.

Initially, the children who participated in the UC Davis study reported feeling "self-conscious," "clumsy," and "uncomfortable" reading out loud. But in the presence of a dog, they felt "more relaxed and confident." They also said the experience was "fun" and "cool."

A child reading to a dog is a concept that is spreading around the world. A few years after the Doctor Dog program began in Hong Kong, Analise Smiley, the education director for Animals Asia, thought up the concept of Professor Paws. "Young children in Hong Kong were learning English but were too embarrassed to speak it out loud in the classroom," explained Jill Robinson. "Dogs are not judgmental and won't criticize a child for getting something wrong, so the children would sit in a circle and practice their English out loud, as if they were speaking to the dogs. Besides improving their English skills, interacting with the dogs also sends an important message of how to live more harmoniously with animals. At the end of the course the children become Pet Cadets and receive a certificate. The process leaves the children feeling empowered, and they go home and teach their parents that dogs are not bad, they are not dirty, and they are our helpers and our friends. Currently three cities in China now have this program integrated in their schools."

This is the power of partnership.

LEARNING TO SAY GOOD-BYE

Do you remember your first? I'm referring to your first cat or dog friend, and the unrivaled connection that relationship brought you. As children, our animals can teach us invaluable qualities, including loyalty, companionship, and love. Their passing may also be the first experience we have with death.

The pain of losing your cat or dog can be just as overwhelming as the loss of a family member or good friend. But unlike many of their human friends, animals seem to accept death with less complexity and greater equanimity.

These final and precious moments give us the opportunity to teach our children how sacred life really is. By engaging in meaningful conversation and allowing feelings to be openly expressed, we can encourage our children not only to care for their beloved friends with kindness, tenderness, and an open heart during their life, but to do so in their last days. The sadness of losing our four-legged friends can break open our hearts and transform us. Our cats and dogs can also bring comfort, hope, and companionship when it's a human who we have loved and lost—as was the case for my stepchildren, Gina and Greg, when Cody, Jester, and I came to visit.

Jester & Gina, Cody & Greg

Years ago, I was divorced and living in Los Angeles with my cats, Jester and Cody, when a miracle happened: I re-met a man that I had known twenty years before during my film editing days, and we fell in love.

Ken lived in Northern California with his two children, ten-year-old Gina and twelve-year-old Greg. Their mother, Lucy, had passed away from breast cancer several years before. Needless to say, the pain of losing a beloved wife and mother had left the entire family feeling bereft.

When the time came to meet Greg and Gina, I packed my suitcase, gifts for both kids, and Cody and Jester into my old Volvo sedan. We drove for seven hours, into the late night, before reaching Ken's home under the pines.

Understandably, when I first arrived, Gina and Greg were curious about my cats, and nervous about me. As Ken showed me around the house, I began to feel like there was something missing. Two young children were living in this home, yet it was strangely quiet. Where was the laughter?

Ken was a sole parent with a full-time job and didn't feel he could care for a dog, though the kids desperately wanted one. As a compromise, he'd brought home a leopard gecko named Splotchy—and Splotchy was loved, but Gina and Greg clearly longed for more.

When Cody and Jester made their entrance and realized they weren't in their cozy apartment anymore, they made a beeline to the couch and hid underneath. Over the next few days (usually close to dinner time), a pink nose would emerge from under the couch or a white paw would swipe a leg passing by. In short order, Jester's antics made him the center of attention. Gina found endless delight in his stealth abilities, and how he chased crumpled paper balls down the stairs and then raced back up with the wad of paper in his mouth. Whenever we played Scrabble, Greg's favorite game, Jester would nestle on Gina's lap and her focus would be completely on him rather than on her game tiles.

As Gina bonded with Jester, I also began to feel her guard coming down with me. Over Jester and a game of Scrabble, the kids and I grew more comfortable around each other, and the odd quiet I'd noticed when I arrived was replaced by our laughter. But unlike Jester, who seemed to have adapted to his new surroundings, Cody remained invisible—preferring his solitude, and the life of a curmudgeon.

Then, one morning, Cody could not be found. Scouring every corner of the house for him, I began to worry that he had somehow slipped out during the night. After more frantic searching, Greg came out of the bedroom, sleepily looked around, and asked what was going on. While we were explaining, a furry yellow head surfaced from under Greg's comforter. Cody! Greg told us that sometime in the night, Cody had jumped up onto his bed and lay purring next to him. He seemed very proud of this distinction, and it was obvious how very special he felt that Cody had chosen him. The smile on that little boy's face was priceless. It still is.

Animals aren't here to replace a parent—they're here to help them. In this ever-changing and often overwhelming world, the presence of a family cat or dog can assist with the physical, mental, and emotional development of kids of every age in countless ways. And the earlier we teach our children about the powerful, health-improving benefits our connection to our animal friends brings, the more likely we are to instill in them healthier and empowering habits that will last their lifetime.

Can we survive without a animal companion in our home? Sure. But by including them in our lives and in our hearts, we can make it more likely that our children will thrive on the ever-challenging road to adulthood.

R

Paws for your Prescription!

From the office of
Nurse Kitty Wiskas and Dr. Harry Friend

1. Do you want to teach your kids responsibility in a fun way? How about dropping by a shelter and bringing one of us home?

2. If your child is ready to care for us and love us, we can't wait! But please choose wisely. Tiny dogs may not be the best fit for an active child, and some kids may connect better with a cat. The point is, we want to be in your home forever. Ask an expert at your local shelter for advice on the best match for your family.

3. We do best and give our best when we share a bedroom with our human friends. Please don't make us sleep outside. Remember, we are your family too!

COMING UP: Now that you've got the kids taken care of, what about you? Cats and dogs can really help make your prime years better than they already are. Here's how . . .

CHAPTER 7

Amazing Adults

"Women and cats will do as they please, and men and dogs should relax and get used to the idea."

—Robert A. Heinlein

As a child, my greatest wish was to become an adult. Today, five decades of life feel like they have shot past me. From college, marriage, divorce, remarriage, parenting, working on movies, and rescuing animals to owning my own business, winning a sexy vegetarian contest, and writing this book, I've had a fun, full and fulfilling life. I'm an adult; there's no arguing with that. In fact, I'm so far into adulthood that my third act is beckoning . . . and it's happening sooner than I anticipated.

Our second act is often our prime; these are the years when most of us burn brightest. It is a time of accomplishment and becoming more aligned with our life's purpose. But adulthood is also a time when life challenges us through illness.

Despite all of the health and wellness information available to us, the Centers for Disease Control and Prevention (CDC) reports that many adults in the US are still making poor lifestyle choices that lead to chronic health issues.

The good news is that life's hiccups can often inspire us to move toward a new and better place; to get there, though, we need a good supply of physical energy and emotional resiliency. A healthy *cattitude* and keen dog sense—inspired by friends of the four-legged variety—can be great assets to get us through the tough times and help us enjoy the great ones.

Today, more people are choosing to live with an animal friend instead of a human one. Cats and dogs often bring into our hectic lives what we are lacking: companionship, a chance to go out in nature and stretch our legs, and unconditional love. These furry companions are scientifically proven stress-busters in perhaps the most stressed-out age that humanity has ever known. Nurture your relationship with them, and a healthier, happier, and more extraordinary life can be your reward.

COLLEGE DAZE

I took my dog to college. Well, at least for the last year. My mom, who was well into her third act, had grown tired of caring for Iris, my shepherd mix, while I was away at school. As I entered my senior year, she threatened to take Iris to the shelter. I loved my dog and was never going to allow her to set one foot in that place, so I practiced my new independence as an adult and got responsible. I found a small house that I could afford (with a roommate who loved dogs), and Iris and I moved in.

If you are lucky enough to have attended college, you know how wonderful it can be to connect with people you wouldn't otherwise meet and be exposed to new ideas you wouldn't otherwise hear—but you also know how stressful the experience can be. For many young people, college life is their first time living away from home, and it can be lonely and isolating. College is not cheap, and graduating with thousands of dollars' worth of debt and no promise of a job can feel like an overwhelming burden for a young adult. Bloomberg *BusinessWeek* reports that depression and anxiety are by far the most prevalent health problems that students of this age confront.[53]

Cats and dogs may not be able to help students pay off their debts or get their dream jobs once they finish school, but thirty minutes of interacting with a cat or a dog each day can do wonders for their mental health during final exam time. Petting an animal promotes the production of human hormones associated with happiness—and cats and dogs seem to like it too. At Yale University, Monty, a therapy dog, can be checked out for thirty minutes at a time. Students have reported that being with Monty soothes them and reminds them of home.[54]

My stepdaughter, Gina, called me from UC Berkeley during her senior year to tell me that Tony La Russa's Animal Rescue Foundation brought dogs to the university's library so the students could pet and play with them during finals week. I asked Gina what it was like. "It was really cool," she said, "and the students really loved it." I could hear the delight in her voice. It is the same voice Gina uses when talking about her own dog, Dakota.

The University of Northern Colorado, The University of Idaho, and the University of Washington are just some of the colleges across the country that are convinced of the benefits that animal companions provide; these colleges allow dogs, cats, hamsters, fish, and other small animals to attend college alongside their favorite students.[55]

Bringing a dog to college can be great fun if you're a student, but it's extremely important that you consider your animal's needs first. Between studying, taking exams, and social engagements, college life imposes severe limits on a student's time and energy. Adopting any animal is a serious decision, and you would never want to give an animal in your care the short end of the stick—or have to relinquish them—because you just don't have time to care for them. So whatever stage of life you are in, please consider their needs before you adopt, because your relationship with them is forever.

CAREER CATS & WORKING DOGS

Now more than ever, cats and dogs are lending us a hand at work. And since many of us also work from home, our furry buddies are helping us there as well. Google, Salesforce, and GoDaddy are just some of the companies that understand the positive influence that animals have on their employees—and that a healthy and happy team member is also a productive one.[56] A 2012 study in the *International Journal of Workplace Health Management* shows that having dogs in the workplace not only lowers stress but also helps to increase employee job satisfaction. Workers tend to bond more with each other and are more relaxed when there's a pooch around. On the flip side, when a dog is left behind at home, the dog is unhappy *and* stress levels rise in their working guardians.[57]

In my own community, EDG Interior Architecture & Design, an international firm with seventy-five employees, allows dog helpers to attend work with their guardians. According to Jeffrey Ho, a junior designer in the company, "Taking breaks and playing with my dog, Buddy, helps relieve my stress, makes me more productive, and even helps me be more creative. He brightens up the workday for everyone in the office, so it's mutually beneficial for everyone."

Another employee, Julia, told me, "Bringing dogs here makes the workplace more comfortable, like home. I recently had to take time to focus on myself and learn how to handle my anxiety and depression. Nothing calms me down more than spending time with a loving animal. Their touch is soothing, and they look at you with nothing but compassion and admiration. All they want is love (and maybe some food). You cannot be stressed around them. To them, you are amazing. Humans can't always make you feel that way."

I know how Julia feels. Back in the days when I didn't have a six-pack of my own, I had to go looking outside home—and work—for the comfort of an animal companion.

Justine & Carlyn

When I was single, cat-less, and working long hours in film editing, I often spent time in the Either/Or Bookstore in Hermosa Beach, California, a sprawling athenaeum with a relaxed, bohemian feel. At Either/Or, everyday people like me browsed shelves alongside comedians like Jay Leno and Roseanne Barr, who performed at the Comedy and Magic Club nearby.

I have always taken great comfort in old books like the ones that lived in this store, but in addition to its tomes, Either/Or had something else—or rather, a special someone else: a black cat named Justine who lived in the store. As I rummaged through the personal development section in search of the book that would help me understand why I was so unlucky in love,

Justine would pop out of some corner and greet me, soliciting a stroke or two and giving me a chirrup for my efforts. She would spend time with me, lying on top of books I shouldn't read, and plopping next to ones she thought I should take a look at.

I loved animals but was too busy at work to care for one. I was also single and hoping for love—and Justine brought me a little joy, a glimmer of possibility, and a welcome reprieve from my worries. You can never know the struggles a person is going through in life, but Justine seemed to sense mine, and she eased them for a time.

The Either/Or Bookstore did not survive the big chain bookstore invasion, and it eventually closed its doors. Justine is long gone now. But I have often thought how wonderful it would be to have an animal friend beside you as you work. Now I've been able to experience that joy firsthand while writing this book with my feline and canine buddies alongside me. In their own unique ways the members of my six-pack have calmed, uplifted, and inspired me daily throughout this journey, just like Justine did all those years ago.

A WOMAN'S BEST FRIEND

Today's world demands more from women than ever before. In the past, a woman's responsibility was to be the primary caregiver for her husband and children. But today, according to a Pew Research analysis, moms in four out of ten American households with children under eighteen are either the sole or primary wage earners for their family.[58]

Getting up early, making meals, driving the kids to soccer practice, cleaning the house, listening to everyone's problems, getting to bed late, then doing it all again the next day . . . a working mom's demands are too many to be listed and often go underappreciated. Unlike Hermione Granger, the brilliant young girl in the *Harry Potter* movies, women do not possess Time-Turners that set back the clock and give us extra hours in the day. We have to do the best we can to balance our family life, our work and our well-being with the limited and precious hours that we do have.

Heart disease was once considered a man's disease, but as the demands placed on women have increased, its incidence has risen in the female population.[59] Diabetes and cancer are also leading causes of death for women today, according to the Centers for Disease Control.[60] Because these conditions are positively affected by a healthy lifestyle, having a cat or a dog in your home can help you copilot your health journey, especially when it comes to exercise and stress reduction.

Generally, once women have children they tend to exercise less and often don't return to the level of activity they were accustomed to prior to becoming a mom.[61] Having a dog buddy can be the encouragement a working mom needs to get out before work for a brisk walk or jog. Even a short walk can get your heart rate moving, make your lungs expand, and strengthen your bones. Plus, along the way you can meet other dog lovers, get a shot of Vitamin D from the morning sun, and enjoy some moments in nature.

Pregnant and menopausal animal lovers also have an advantage: During pregnancy, women are more likely to meet recommended exercise levels by walking their dogs than are pregnant woman in households without a canine.[62] And after your child-bearing years, when the hot flashes come a-calling, taking your dog for a stroll can be a better symptom reliever than standing in front of an open freezer—as can doing those yoga stretches that your cat is so good at modeling for you.[63]

Widowed women who live with animal companions also have been shown to experience significantly fewer of the negative physical and psychological symptoms associated with disease and aging. In contrast to widows who did not have animal friends living beside them, these women also reported taking less medications.[64]

Anytime cortisol, our stress hormone, can be replaced with oxytocin and serotonin, the hormones that make us feel happy and loved, we need to jump on the opportunity. Cats and dogs provide us with many of these moments. The positive side effects of these interactions can be as long as the list of negative side effects on a prescription drug commercial—the difference, of course, being that feeling more calm, balanced, and happy through our animal-human connection is beneficial, not harmful. Dog doctors and cat nurses certainly are a girl's best friends—just ask Marie, who transformed her life with a *Smalls* dose of love.

Smalls & Marie

When I was in my early twenties, I worked in a veterinarian's office in San Francisco, California. One day, a mother cat and her eight kittens were brought in. The kittens were really sick with respiratory issues, eye infections, and ringworm. With medical care, though, they all improved—except for the smallest one, whom I named Smalls.

Because Smalls was a quiet kitty that always slept at the bottom of the kitten pile, he wasn't getting enough milk from his mother, so I began to bottle-feed him. He was a Seal Point Burmese, but he didn't look like one because he was bald, blind, and covered in ringworm lesions. Although his littermates were being adopted, no one wanted Smalls because he looked so sickly. When his last sibling, a sister, was taken from the cage they shared, Smalls wailed inconsolably. As I listened to him cry, I could feel how alone and frightened he felt, so I agreed to take him. I tucked him in my shirt and started keeping him near me all of the time. Smalls and I would ride the bus to work together; he'd wait at the vet's office while I finished my shift; and then we'd go home together at night.

Smalls needed me, but the truth is, I needed him more. I was trying to change my life. I had been a wild kid, and had made a lot of trouble for myself in my early adulthood. I was trying to lead a straighter life, to maintain a steady job, and to take better care of myself. I wanted to make these changes, but because I was very shy, angry, and felt defensive toward other people, I was having difficulty. Smalls was the perfect teacher for me, at the perfect time, because he showed me a better way.

As I took care of Smalls, I noticed that no matter how many times we poked him with a needle, made him take a bath, or subjected him to some kind of medical treatment, he was always cheerful, good-natured, and gentle. I decided to model myself after Smalls. When I was faced with a difficult situation I would ask myself, "What would Smalls do?"

I wasn't well cared for when I was growing up, and as a consequence I needed others to validate me so I could feel better about myself. Smalls didn't have a great beginning either, and there were all sorts of reasons for him to lash out or be untrusting, but he never would. He was loving, and fearless. Smalls taught me how my behavior affected other people's reactions toward me. If I was more upbeat and outgoing, like Smalls, people would respond positively to me, and that would make me feel good.

As I became more affable, I also began to feel less angry toward others. Loving and caring for Smalls made me more loving with myself, and it gave me a greater purpose in life.

As Smalls' health improved, his vision also returned, and he became a beautiful little cat. We blossomed together—and neither one of us could have done it alone. He needed my companionship, my love, and the safety I offered him; and I needed him as my teacher. Even though he was a small and defenseless creature, he helped me so much more than I helped him. By caring for Smalls, I learned to care for myself, and now I walk more gently in the world.

MAN'S BEST FRIEND

A study was conducted at the University of Buffalo to find out whether having a companion cat or dog would make a difference to a person's blood pressure. The study was done on one of the most stressed-out groups of people alive today: New York stockbrokers. All of the participants were taking blood pressure–lowering medication when the study began.

The results? Stockbrokers with a cat or dog had more stable cardiovascular health during stressful situations than their colleagues in the control group who did not live with an animal companion. According to one of the researchers, "When we told the group that didn't have pets about the findings, many went out and got them."[65]

Heart disease is the leading cause of death worldwide for men, and in the US, one in four will die from it.[66] This disease is often preventable with a plant-based diet, regular exercise, and by managing stress levels— all areas that our animal friends can help us with. For the same reasons that a cat or dog companion can benefit a woman's health in her prime of life, the same is true for men. If you read Steve's story about Gus, you'll understand what I mean.

Gus & Steve

We went to Animal Control to adopt a cat and found an orange tabby in the back of a cage with a big sticker that warned, "heart murmur!" The name on his cage said, "Shy," but this cat was anything but. As soon this kitty saw us, he started rolling around, wanting us to play with him. The heart murmur warning didn't deter us for a second. My partner K.C. and I decided this little guy was coming home with us. We named our new friend Gus.

Gus was like a dog: he loved to follow us everywhere in the house, including to the downstairs mailbox. He was a type A cat with a lot of energy, but he also enjoyed relaxing.

Over time, Gus developed diabetes, and we began to give him injections twice a day, which he accepted without complaint. Whenever I'd get a cold or the flu, Gus and I would snuggle in bed and get better together. He loved to lie across my chest and curl up under my neck, sometimes spending hours there. We took care of Gus, but Gus also took very good care of us.

Gus even fueled my imagination as VP of Development for the PETA Foundation. He had an uncanny ability to get from the floor to the center of a table using a series of steps to leverage himself up and get what he wanted (which was to be in command of whichever room he happened to be in, and to keep an eye on everything that went on). After observing this skill, I was inspired to create a presentation where I talked about applying the laws of physics to fundraising.

In my job, I see images and situations of animal cruelty on a daily basis. Sharing this information with the public to educate and bring awareness about the pain and suffering of animals can be very stressful. I remember an investigation that we conducted at the University of Wisconsin involving an orange tabby named Double Trouble who had been forced to endure cruel experiments by researchers. I would arrive home after a long day of looking at these images and Gus, who looked a lot like Double Trouble, would be there to greet me. Coming home to someone with whom I had such a strong connection, and who represented those I was fighting to make a better world for, made me more resolved to work harder at what I *do. Gus's resilience in bouncing back time after time from his diabetes also inspired me to push forward and fight injustice, no matter what challenges I faced.*

Gus was like my nurse. I looked forward to getting home every night and throwing my legs over the side of a chair. He would lie on my chest, purring, and in this way he would directly send me his calming energy. Because of him, I have learned to slow down and be present with those that I love. It was a magical and beautiful time that we had together. Gus was the love of my life.

In December, Gus started to lose weight and we were told that he had kidney cancer. Thankfully, he wasn't in pain and didn't suffer. We stayed with him until he passed away. On the same day, my colleague in India adopted a cat who had been left outside in the cold weather in Mumbai. The cat had given birth to kittens but only one had survived. She sent me a picture of him, an orange tabby—and he was the spittin' image of Gus!

My friend named her kitty Mango. I like to think that Gus's life is carrying on through this little being and that the energy, care, and love that Gus gave to me is now being given to my friend. I hope that Mango is bringing peace to her world, just like Gus brought peace to mine.

Paws for your Prescription!

From the office of
Nurse Kitty Wiskas and Dr. Harry Friend

1. If you can, why not adopt a furry friend for a healthier and happier prime of life?

2. We may not be able to come to college with you but we'd sure love a visit from you while we're waiting at a shelter for our forever homes. You could take a dog for a walk, or visit us kitties in our play areas. We can even help you relax before finals.

3. Can we come to work with you? Talk to your employer about the health benefits, then bring us by for a visit to see if it's a good fit for your workplace *and* for us.

COMING UP: Cats and dogs can positively affect us at every stage of life, even as we move toward our best act yet: our third act.

CHAPTER 8

Sensational Seniors

"All his life he tried to be a good person. Many times, however, he failed. For after all, he was only human. He wasn't a dog."

—Charles M. Schulz

America is aging. By 2050, nearly eighty million people will be sixty-five years of age or older.[67] And if you're one of those eighty million, here's the hard truth: as you move into your third act, you will encounter health-related issues with greater frequency. Besides cosmetic changes—wrinkles, gray hair, sagging skin—people over sixty are also faced with physiological challenges: difficulty balancing, blurred vision, poor memory, and pain.

Aging is inevitable; for many people, however, poor health is something that we can take measures to prevent. Staying socially active, learning new things, and maintaining a sense of purpose and appreciation for life also contribute greatly to a lengthy third act. Add a healthy dose of humor, and we will be seeing you on planet earth for a good long time!

Who do you know who can encourage you to participate in many of these ageless aging activities better than cats or dogs? If there was ever a time to develop a strong and mutually beneficial relationship with a four-legged companion, your third act is it!

THE PERKS OF FOUR-LEGGED COMPANIONSHIP

According to a 1999 study in the *Journal of American Geriatrics*, older people living with animal companions enjoy better physical and emotional health than those without. Dog guardians also have longer life spans.[68] And those aren't the only perks that await a senior who shares their home with an animal friend.

7 PERKS OF AN ANIMAL-FILLED THIRD ACT

- Improved ability to cope with stress
- Fewer doctor visits
- Reduced blood pressure and improved heart health
- Better weight maintenance
- Higher self-esteem
- Less depression
- Shorter hospital stays

One of the biggest keys to healthy aging is eating well; the problem is that as the years pass, a weaker sense of taste and smell can diminish our appetites. Cats and dogs can help us find renewed joy in our food. When recipients of the Meals on Wheels program were allowed to eat near their animals, for example, their eating patterns improved. Meals on Wheels volunteers noticed that seniors were even feeding their cats and dogs from their own plates, so they began bringing food for the animals too.[69]

Caring for an animal friend can keep an older person active. Walking, feeding, grooming, and playing with an animal stimulates physical and mental activity. Exercising with our dogs and stretching with our cats contributes to a healthy heart and puts our ligaments and joints to good use. Walking with our canine friends strengthens our bones, which otherwise become brittle as we age. And even close friends are no substitute for a dog; older people are actually more likely to take regular walks if their walking companions are canine rather than human.[70]

A perfect example of this phenomenon comes from Margaret Holiday, an animal and human chiropractor working in the San Francisco Bay Area, whose client Anne felt her walking days were over—until her chow chow, Frederick, insisted they were not.

Frederick & Anne

Anne was elderly and was having trouble with her balance. Her doctor told her she needed to go for a walk every single day but because she felt unstable, she insisted that walking was something she could no longer do at her age.

Finally, Anne called me to talk about this issue, and we discussed how walking with Frederick, her chow chow, might help her bring mobility back into her life again.

Anne was open to the idea of walking with Frederick, but she lived on a steep hill and was concerned that if her fifty-pound dog saw a squirrel or other distraction, he might pull her down, injuring her in the process. So Anne bought a special harness that allowed her to attach Frederick to her waistband. We also decided it would be better for her and Frederick to walk uphill rather than downhill so Anne could have greater control as they began to walk together.

We started with a five-minute walk two times a day. Little by little, the walking duration increased, and soon Anne was walking for forty-five minutes—twice a day.

Because of Fredrick, Anne's life has totally changed. Before, she had such limited mobility that she had problems just walking around inside her home. Her daily walks with Frederick have gotten her to exercise and helped her lose weight; she is even off of her diabetes medication. Walking with Frederick is no longer the scary thing it once was for Anne, and their partnership has brought her a renewed and unexpected confidence. Her doctor is so happy he's told Anne he wishes he could clone Frederick because then he might be able to help a lot of other people, too.

For a member of the Third Act Club, the benefits of an animal companion aren't just limited to physical well-being; they are also a source of emotional nourishment. Growing older can isolate a person, especially when they have a disability that makes it difficult for them to connect with other people. Fortunately, cats and dogs act as social magnets. According to some studies, disabled people in wheelchairs who are accompanied by a service dog have an average of eight friendly approaches from strangers, versus one approach without a dog.[71]

In elderly living facilities, having a dog doctor or cat nurse making the rounds makes the residents happier and creates better interactions between them.

As we age, loss becomes a greater part of our experience. In our youth, it's easy to take our bodies for granted and hard to imagine the loss of function and vitality that may come in our senior years. Then there's the even harder loss of family and friends, the frequency of which increases as we age. Cats and dogs can be a great comfort during these lonely times—and they are often a senior's only friend. Caring for an animal friend gives a senior a good reason to get out of bed each day, face the world, and find joy in life's precious moments.

AN AGELESS ICON

Does it feel to you as if the world no longer values people past a certain age? Our elders were once revered as the keepers of knowledge and wisdom, but modern culture often places greater value on youth, speed, and celebrity rather than on the richness of life experience.

Because of this, I am always impressed when I see someone defy expectation, break the mold, and harness the power that age brings. Dr. Elliot Katz, the founder and President Emeritus of In Defense Of Animals (IDA), an international organization dedicated to ending the abuse and exploitation of animals, is one of those people.

During my interview with Dr. Katz, his charming Staffordshire terrier, Charlie, joined us. Charlie's warm muzzle lay on my lap as his guardian shared stories about his life and work.

"From the time I was a child, I identified with the plight of the underdog, with those who were weak and vulnerable, exploited and abandoned," Dr Katz told me. "When I was eight years old I vowed to become a veterinarian after a little dog that I rescued gave birth to six puppies. One after the other, all of the puppies died from distemper, despite everything that my father and I did to save their lives. When I realized the terrible suffering these puppies had to go through and the tragedy of their deaths, my future opened up to me. I decided to become a guardian to the most vulnerable, and to protect them from exploitation and cruelty."

With Dr. Katz at the helm, IDA has achieved many victories on behalf of animals: opening a sixty-four-acre sanctuary for abandoned animals in rural Mississippi, developing a forest sanctuary in Cameroon, fighting the puppy mill industry, and launching successful campaigns against vivisection are just some of their accomplishments.

In his eighties, Dr. Katz's voice on behalf of animals is going stronger than ever with the Guardian Campaign. This growing movement encourages people to use the term "guardian" instead of "owner" when describing their relationships with their animal companions. The mindset behind the campaign is that the term "animal owner" implies that your animal is property, a commodity, or a possession, whereas "animal guardian" suggests that you value your relationship with your animal friends beyond the concept of property and with greater respect, compassion, and kindness.

Can words really be that important? Science says yes! Drs. Pamela Carlisle-Frank and Joshua Frank examined the attitudes of animal guardians and pet owners, and their study revealed that people who consider themselves "animal guardians" are more likely to think of their four-legged companions as family members and are less likely to abandon them than are people who consider themselves "pet owners."[72] This is significant, since 2.7 million abandoned cats and dogs are euthanized in our nation's shelters every year.[73]

After my interview with Dr. Katz, I felt inspired and embraced being an animal guardian. What happened next was unexpected: I found that embodying the term *guardian* soon transcended my relationship with my cats and dogs and spread to other areas of my life. As a stepparent, being a guardian gives me greater clarity in my role with my husband's children than the confusing term "stepparent" ever allowed. Bringing the idea of guardianship to my relationship with my husband reminds me to take care of someone I consider priceless and often take for granted. And finally, as a planetary guardian, I've become a more conscious citizen of the world, taking greater care to leave a smaller carbon footstep whenever I can.

Cats and dogs inspire us to stay healthy at all three stages of life, and as Dr. Katz's story proves, you are never too young or too old to change the world.

Paws for your Prescription!

From the office of
Nurse Kitty Wiskas and Dr. Harry Friend

1. Do you need some incentive to get out and about? Do you want to change your wrinkles to laugh lines? Would you like to make a new friend who is grateful for every little thing you do? Look no further; we're your best medicine.

2. A puppy is adorable for sure, but just because we're a little gray doesn't mean we aren't just as eager to give you all of our friendship and love. When adopting, please don't forget us old guys.

3. Do you think you're too old to do something extraordinary? Can you write a book? Volunteer your time? Mentor someone? If there is something you've always wanted to do but haven't quite gotten around to it? Well, now is the time.

4. Are you remembering to visit the *Dog as My Doctor, Cat as My Nurse* online photo gallery? If not, stop by for a visit and meet everyone that you've been reading about at www.AnimalHumanHealth.com/gallery/.

COMING UP: Physical health is a vital element of longevity, but it isn't everything. We are also composed of an emotional-mental body that's just as important as the physical one—and often even more essential. Can cats and dogs enhance our emotional lives? If you're an animal lover, I think you know the answer to that one.

PART II

Your Happy Mind

If a dog were my doctor or a cat my nurse,
what advice would they give me?

"Both by direct communication and by example, my animal companions are always acting as my guardians. The message that is most often sent? 'Slow Down.' There is nothing on your plate today that is more important than a few moments of being here. Being present. Being grounded. Just being."

—Jackson Galaxy, cat behaviorist and host of the television show *My Cat from Hell*

CHAPTER 9

The Magic in Mindfulness

"That was Zen, this is meow."

—Anonymous

Have you ever visited the Land of *Now*? For many of us, the *Now*—in other words, the exact moment you are in—can be as impossible to reach as the Land of Oz. The majority of humans tend to live in one of two preferred realities: the past or the future. But in truth, since the past no longer exists and the future has yet to come, the only reality we truly have is right now (even though many of us find it hard to visit there for more than a few moments at a time).

How often do you get somewhere and realize you don't even remember *how* you got there? That's the *Now* escaping you, and it happens when you are stressed out and feeling overwhelmed. Each day, many of us work more than one job to make ends meet; we get pulled in opposite directions by family and career; and we live in a hurried, stressed, and anxious haze. At the end of the day, we embrace the sofa and TV like they're much-needed lovers, often at the expense of connecting with flesh-and-blood lovers or our family (you know, those people who actually live alongside you in the *Now*).

Getting lost in thoughts of the past or future is one way we avoid the present moment; our chronic use of cell phones, computers, and tablets is another. Technology is not the enemy—quite the opposite, digital devices have made our lives easier in countless ways—but it does contribute to our lack of connection to what is actually going on around us. How many times have you gone to dinner with a group of people only to find half of them checking their voicemails or texting their friends? Many states have laws against driving while using a cell phone, yet not a day goes by that I don't notice someone driving with a phone at their ear as they navigate through traffic.

If you are someone who regularly sits down to check your e-mail while texting your wife, and while simultaneously glancing at the news, here's something to ponder: your brain can only focus on one thing at a time.

Research at Stanford University shows that people who regularly engage in multitasking use their brains less effectively and cannot recall information as well as those who concentrate on one thing at a time.[74] Basically, when you try to get everything done at once, you're probably being about as efficient as an eight-year-old child.[75]

It is challenging to unplug in this modern world of artificial devices and accelerated living. But if we are to thrive in the midst of the technological onslaught we're experiencing today, it's in our best interest to find ways to disengage with distraction and reengage with ourselves. Fortunately, humankind is starting to catch on by embracing the *Now* with a simple and timeless approach: mindfulness. Something our cats and dogs know just a little bit about.

THE ART OF NOTICING

Jon Kabat-Zinn, Professor Emeritus at University of Massachusetts Medical School and the founder of Mindfulness Based Stress Reduction (MBSR), defines mindfulness as "the awareness that arises from paying attention on purpose, in the present moment, without judgment or reaction to whatever appears in your field of experience."

Besides increasing your efficiency and productivity, mindfulness can help you become less stressed, reduce chronic pain, and decrease your blood pressure.[76] Dr. Kabat-Zinn has successfully used mindfulness techniques for over twenty years to help people living with chronic pain find a greater quality of life.

How do you practice mindfulness? Start paying attention to what you are doing at any time, no matter what it is. Bring all five of your senses—sight, smell, touch, taste, and hearing—to whatever task you are engaged in right now. As you wash the dishes, become aware of how the warm, soapy water feels on your hands. When you talk with your partner, gently bring your attention to their voice and focus on what they are saying instead of letting your thoughts drift to yesterday's conversation with your mother. As you drive, bring your awareness to the feel of the steering wheel under your hands and the color of the stoplight ahead. We may not have the option of creating more time in our hectic lives, but we can expand the time we have by being present in our environment, with each other, and with ourselves. The *Now* is all around us, and everything that's truly important exists in that space.

MASTERS OF MINDFULNESS

Remaining mindful in a world that constantly tempts you with distraction may sound difficult or even impossible. But, like riding a bike, learning to cook plant-based meals, or trying out a new exercise, mindfulness is a skill we can develop. The more we engage the mindfulness muscle, the better we get at it. Mindfulness teachers abound—and if you're an animal lover, you don't need to go out looking for one; the best teacher you'll ever find probably needs their ears scratched by their favorite student just about now.

Below are a few ways that you and your cat and dog friends can enjoy some moments of mindfulness together. Let's see if you can be as focused, and as delighted in the *Now,* as they are.

MINDFUL MOMENTS WITH CATS & DOGS

- Feeling your cat's weight, warmth, and intoxicating purring as he lies on you.
- Brushing your cat or dog's fur with gentle and mindful strokes.
- Taking time to carefully check their bodies for lumps and bumps, and to remove burrs.

- Walking your dog with a greater awareness of the sights and sounds around you.
- Engaging your cat or dog in your morning ritual.

Living in the present moment helps you slow down, and it also takes your mind away from the worries of yesterday and those of tomorrow. These mindful moments spread into the rest of your life, enriching your relationships, enhancing your creativity, and making life more harmonious. They can also deepen the bonds you have with a certain four-legged friend who would enjoy nothing more than spending quality time with the human they love most, even when that human is sick—as in the following story of a mother's unwavering love and a dog named Arlo.

Arlo, Anne Marie & Constance

On October 2013, the unthinkable happened. My beautiful and vibrant daughter, Anne Marie, was diagnosed with stage IV colon cancer. The disease had metastasized to her liver, and the doctors gave her between six months and a year to live. Two days after her diagnosis, Anne Marie had a permanent port installed in her chest and the doctors began her on chemotherapy treatments.

I felt helpless watching Anne Marie surrounded by the harshness of the clinical setting. Week after week she lay hooked up to IVs, having multiple drugs pumped into her body, as white coats hovered over and around her. At the end of the treatments she would be so medicated that she could hardly get out of my car and into her own bed. I knew the medications were meant to stabilize the tumors, but after each new round of chemo, she would suffer for five to six days with a nausea that seemed to have no end. Perhaps what was even harder to witness was the grey pallor that came over her skin after those treatments. It was as if her life force was diminishing before my eyes.

Anne Marie is not only my daughter, she is a wife, sister, and mother to two very young children. It is nearly impossible for our family to wrap our hearts and heads around her diagnosis and the thought of losing her. The only bright light that seems to shine through these dark times is my younger daughter's dog, an Australian cattle dog named Arlo.

One weekend, after I had just finished walking Arlo, Anne Marie called me. She had just received her infusion, and asked me to bring Arlo with me on my visit. This was unexpected. I usually leave Arlo behind when I go see her. But she had her heart so set on seeing him that I brought him along. When we arrived at her house, Arlo ran inside and over to Anne Marie and jumped on her bed. He lay on top of her, his head plopped on her lap.

"Honey, is that okay?" I asked, a bit worried that he might upset her. But I needn't have been concerned.

"Yes!" she said and wrapped her arms around his body, melting into him. As his golden eyes enveloped her, Anne Marie's energy completely changed, and the greyness around her dissipated. It was as if in Arlo's presence, Anne Marie was coming to life.

Arlo is very sensitive to Anne Marie when she is feeling bad, but he doesn't allow her to be in that low space for too long. He looks into her face with those amazing eyes, licks her, or lies on top of her, bringing his innocence and an attitude that says, "The world is a wonderful place!" Petting Arlo calms and soothes Anne Marie in a way that nothing else can; Arlo brings her hope.

As a parent, seeing that your child isn't feeling well makes you want to try everything possible to make things right. In this situation, there is so little I can do. I can't take away Anne Marie's nausea, or her pain, or give her the energy to get out of bed. I feel there is nothing I can do to bring her aliveness back except to be with her, love her, and bring Arlo over for visits.

Arlo isn't just a great comfort to Anne Marie; he gets my focus off of things that I cannot change. Because he needs me to take care of him, take him outside, and feed him, he provides me with an opportunity to set aside my sadness and frustration, and the helplessness I feel in my inability to make things different. Arlo gets me moving even when I feel like I'd rather not. I take him for long walks up and down the streets in San Francisco, and I always feel better afterward.

My love for my daughter is indescribable, and sometimes I'm afraid that my love will overwhelm her. Arlo doesn't care what anyone thinks, though—he shows up with all of himself in any given moment and puts his *full being into whatever space he's in. Arlo lives in the Now, and he doesn't hold back; he loves without condition. If that is too much for anyone and he is asked to move into the living room, he goes without complaint. Arlo isn't afraid of rejection or of fully being all of who he is in every moment.*

When I see this I realize it's okay for me to show up and throw my arms around Anne Marie and tell her how much I love her. I can allow her to decide for herself if she does or doesn't want my affection. Arlo reminds me to not be afraid of being who I am, of showing all of the love I have to give, and all that I have to share.

It's been three years since Anne Marie received her six-month prognosis. Yesterday we got the results from her CT scan. "STABLE," they said. The future is uncertain, but right now, life is full of love and hope. And Arlo is here to remind us of that.

Just by being himself, Arlo gave Constance the gift of experiencing the present in a deeper and more meaningful way. But how much further can our animal friends take us into the Land of *Now*?

After my experience with Cesar Millan and his dogs (described in Chapter 4), I began to learn how sensitive animals are to their human guardian's energy. Through this special connection, our animals invite us to become aware of our feelings, and, if we choose, to transform those energies into a more balanced state. If that isn't amazing enough, my animals took my education one step further by showing me what it feels like to be in "The Zone," which is basically a heightened sense of the *Now*.

Roxy, Cesar & Carlyn: Part II

When I took Roxy to Cesar Millan for help with her aggression issues, I didn't realize that our afternoon together would change Roxy's life . . . and mine. In Chapter 4, I shared with you how Cesar taught me that Roxy could feel my energy and sense my mood. If I was stressed or anxious, Roxy knew it and would react—usually aggressively. I knew that if Roxy was ever to have a chance of remedying her behavioral issues, I would have to change my energy, my nervousness, and my irritability.

After the workshop, Roxy and I made our way to a remote area of the horse ranch, where Cesar and his dogs were waiting for us in an outdoor corral. Well over a dozen rottweilers, pit bulls, and other assorted street dogs swarmed inside the enclosure. I have never been afraid of dogs, but as we approached, the primal rumbling that came from the collective made the hairs on my arm bristle. Roxy, a street dog herself, usually walked with a healthy strut and confident gaze, but today her ribs were glued against my leg. I laid my hand on her head for comfort, but compared to this pack, Roxy looked like a Park Avenue debutante.

When Cesar led Roxy into the corral, she let it be known that she was not there to make friends: she growled and lunged at the other dogs. But even in the face of her fearful aggression, they all maintained a calm and curious demeanor. I knew from the workshop I'd attended earlier that day that they were being influenced by Cesar's own calm energy.

It took about twenty minutes for Roxy, the dog that everyone in the afternoon workshop had considered to be the most aggressive, to begin to play with dogs that moments earlier she had wanted to attack. As I watched my girl soliciting play from her dog peers, my eyes began to mist for the second time that day. I couldn't tell you what changed for Roxy. To the naked eye, nothing had really happened. But energy is not usually apparent to the naked eye—not to mine, at least.

For the next hour, Cesar, the dogs, and I hiked the hilly landscape around the horse ranch. Beside us and behind us were thirty dogs, including Roxy, who walked steadfastly at our side. As we walked, there was no place we had to be, no phones needing answering, no other distractions to pull us away from the moment we were in. Eventually we fell into a silent, rhythmic state of movement—an effortless ease—with all of us, dogs and humans, walking as one. I began to tune into the palate of greens and earthy browns surrounding me, to feel the rocky ground under my sneakers; and my heart began to beat in sync with the symphony of dog paws thudding gently alongside us. My tension dissipated, and calm settled into my mind. Even focus itself became lost in the moment. We were in what Cesar calls "The Zone."

The Zone is a heightened state of the *Now*—what Japanese martial artists call "Mushin" and psychology calls "flow." It is the feeling of complete immersion where you become so engrossed in what you're doing that you lose track of everything else that's going on around you. Athletes, musicians, and painters experience this when they become so focused on the one thing they're doing that they stop *doing* it and begin to *become* it.

You don't have to be an athlete or an artist to enter The Zone. You can get there by washing your car, brushing your teeth, or lying with your cat. You can get there by engaging in mindfulness; and you can arrive at mindfulness at any moment by becoming aware of what you are doing in that instant.

After our walk with Cesar and his dogs, I took Roxy to the beach for the sunset. As we watched the sun disappear together, I felt a greater sense of clarity and a deeper connection to her.

I have found myself in The Zone a few times since that day—while doing yoga, writing this book, and even giving acupuncture treatments—but that first time was unforgettable. Since that day, I've strived to have a more mindful partnership with all my animals. And I'm always looking forward to my next visit to The Zone.

Paws for your Prescription!

From the office of
Nurse Kitty Wiskas and Dr. Harry Friend

1. How can you be more mindful today? If you are stuck for an answer, check in with your feline nurse—we are in the present moment pretty much all of the time.

2. Let's do one of the mindful moments listed earlier in this chapter together. Or, if you prefer, let's come up with one of our very own.

3. Shall we go for a long walk today and see if we stumble across The Zone . . . or at least a bone?

COMING UP: Just by noticing a little bit more each day, you have discovered the present and arrived at the Land of Now. Let's go one step further and dive into the power of your thoughts.

CHAPTER 10

The Power of Thought

"Once you have had a wonderful dog,
a life without one is a life diminished."

—Dean Koontz

When I was eleven I thought myself straight into a hospital bed.

One morning, with great enthusiasm, my fifth-grade teacher announced that our annual "Spring Sing" for parents and guests would be in two weeks. The performance would consist of our class singing an old-fashioned row-row-row-your-boat type of song on stage. Projected behind us would be larger-than-life photographs of boy and girl couples wearing clothing from the turn of the century and sitting in a rowboat together.

I was coupled with a cute boy who I had a mad crush on and who shall remain nameless, since he actually went on to have great fame as an athlete in his adult years. Wearing our Sawyeresque clothing, nameless boy and I sat in the boat, shyly averting our eyes from each other's gaze. Caught between nervousness and excitement, I laughed the moment the teacher said "cheese"—not a cute, delicate laugh but a loud, raucous one.

I had no idea how unattractive that laugh made me look until days later, when the photo was projected onto a large screen in front of my classmates. The kids roared and my cheeks burned red and hot as I sat at my desk staring into the enormous mouth of Jonah the Whale Montes

De Oca. Realizing this humiliating image would be shown to an auditorium full of strangers left me even more stunned.

After class, I begged my teacher to take another picture. To this day I remember her head moving slowly back and forth: no mercy. And she was either a good guesser or a mind-reader, because the next day she announced to the class that the only acceptable excuse for missing the Spring Sing would be if we ended up in the hospital. She couldn't have known how powerful that suggestion would be.

A few days later I caught a cold, the cold became the flu and the flu turned into acute asthma. My struggle for breath became so severe I ended up in the hospital, and (not so sadly) missed the Spring Sing.

Thus, at a very early age, I learned that my thoughts held an invisible power, and that this power is available to anyone—even an eleven-year-old child.

THE MIND-BODY CONNECTION

From childhood onward we spend countless hours, days, and years cultivating our thoughts—many of them negative in nature. Our thoughts reflect our perception of other people's actions, the environment around us, and even ourselves. I viewed my Spring Sing photo as embarrassing and even shameful, but another child with a different frame of mind might have laughed out loud with their classmates.

Our thoughts give rise to our feelings and emotions. Negative emotions, like a burst of anger, grief over the loss of a loved one, or frustration when something repeatedly goes wrong, are normal. When they continually spin in our heads, however, they can give rise to physical manifestations. A motorist cuts you off in traffic, and *Irresponsible jerk!* flashes through your mind as your blood pressure rises. Your child gets into a fight at school, and you get so anxious that you can't sleep. In the morning you feel exhausted. Someone you love dies, and as you begin to think of all of the people you care about who you will one day lose, your head begins to throb.

Often we fail to notice the connection between our physical experience and the thoughts that live beneath them. But if we want to prevent illness, to understand what may lie at the root of what ails us, or to live a long and healthy life, it would serve us to look at the thought patterns that might be contributing to our physical symptoms. In other words, we need to be aware of the power that exists in the mind-body connection.

Headaches, chest pain, and digestive issues are some of the physical challenges that come from our thoughts and the resulting stress they can produce in the body. If you are reliving traumas, ensconced in fear-based thoughts, or feeling stressed about the future, your physical body is also producing a physical response, as if whatever you are thinking about is occurring right now. According to research, replaying our negative thoughts is so powerful it can even change our DNA.[77]

NEGATIVE THOUGHT BUSTERS

We all have negative thoughts from time to time. But if you find you are spending a lot of time feeling envious of your coworker's promotion and not enough time enjoying your two- and four-legged family, then you might want to take advantage of the following five ways that your cats and dogs can help shift your thoughts into a more positive space.

1. Distraction in Action

Your boss is hinting "layoff" unless you put in longer hours without extra pay. You get to your new car and realize someone has backed into it. On your way home you get a call from your girlfriend, and instead of saying "happy birthday," she says, "I want to break up." What a day!

You get home and stumble over to the couch. You sit there, feeling your heart pounding and your head aching. Then you turn and see your dog standing beside you with a ball in her mouth. It's impossible to focus on two thoughts at once, so this is your chance to turn things around. Rather than dwelling on all the bad stuff, you can consciously choose to change your thoughts and free your mind through distraction.

Listen to your dog's silent instructions and get up! Step into your yard and take five minutes to throw a ball, toss a Frisbee, or fling a nylon bone for your buddy. Focus on your throw, feel the night air on your skin, and borrow your dog's enthusiasm until you can find some of your own. With every throw, allow your day to diminish, your thoughts to soften, and your mind to enjoy the play. You may not rid yourself of every thought from your challenging day, but these moments of distraction help diffuse the charge. In this moment, everything is perfect for her . . . and for you.

Repeat often.

2. Superpowers Revisited

A week later, your boss fires you, your car battery dies, and you get a call from your girlfriend saying she wants the cat.

"Can't I get a break?!" you shout to no one in particular.

You get home and throw the ball with your dog. It helps, but today, it's not enough. You plop onto the couch and your mind begins its chatter: you're not good enough, not smart enough, and no one loves you.

Never fear; Supercat is here! Your feline friend crawls out from under the couch and jumps on your lap to reassure you that someone does indeed think you are the cat's meow. And your cat friend, unlike your girlfriend, has *three* superpowers: petting, placement, and purring.

Take a few inhales and exhales and prepare for nirvana as you gently pet your kitty with mindful strokes. You know you're doing it right when he slinks back and forth, asking you for more. Feel his warmth and comfort as he settles onto your chest and lies over your heart. As you find yourself relaxing, his purring takes you to another level, away from the stresses of the day. After a few minutes of this, you decide to keep the cat and forget the girlfriend.

3. Groovin' By Movin'

You've been unemployed for two weeks. You had to sell your car for rent money, and your girlfriend took all your furniture. But you still have your sneakers, your cat, and your beloved dog, who insists that you take her for a walk twice a day (or more, since you have some extra time on your hands).

As you breathe in the fresh air and bring oxygen into every part of your body, you begin to realize that life isn't so bad. You didn't like your job much to begin with, and the time away has forced you to send applications to your dream companies. You begin to entertain the possibility of doing something more with your life. And what about love? Well, there is a girl with a labradoodle that you pass on your walk every day . . .

4. The Happy List

You've been distracting your mind on your walks with your dog and using your cat's superpowers to help you relax. Suddenly you get a call to interview for a position at the eco-friendly company of your dreams. You're feeling on top of the world.

However, before you get too settled, and the challenges of the previous weeks become a distant memory, remember that the one thing you can count on is that life is ever-changing. Like a pendulum, highs and lows will visit us for the rest of our lives. Still, we don't have to surrender to those tumultuous swings back and forth. Our strongest defense against life's challenges is to change our perceptions of, and consequently our reactions to, the events that occur around us.

There are many tools to help us with this process, but one of my favorites is "The Happy List." When you are feeling challenged, reaching for your happy list can help you take the edge off by allowing you to remember happier times. The best time to make this list is when you are actually feeling happy. You will need paper and pen, a timer, and a quiet spot. Set the timer for ten minutes, then quickly begin to list all of the things that make you happy. No judging, criticizing, or censoring is allowed; just keep your hand moving, and don't stop writing for the entire ten minutes. If your mind goes blank, just write X's and O's until you come up with something.

Our cats and dogs don't need much to be happy. Their pleasure is a great model for us to remember that joy can come in small packages. What can you do with your animal friends that will encourage you into a better-feeling place? How about . . .

- Watching a funny movie on the couch with your cat.
- Listening to, and singing along with, your favorite songs as you and your dog take a drive to somewhere new.
- Re-reading your favorite childhood book while your cat perches on your back.

- Planning a vacation getaway to a dog-friendly locale.
- Letting your cat pounce on your toes as you slide them back and forth under the bedcovers.
- Visiting a local shelter and taking a lonely dog for a walk, or playing with some of the resident cats who are waiting for adoption. There's nothing like helping others to forget about your own troubles for a while.

Of course, there are many things that you can add to your list that don't involve your companions, and those can be added too. Add to your list often and frequently, and when life comes back at you with a challenge or two, your Happy List and your animal friends will be there to remind you that this, too, shall pass.

5. Think and Grow Paws-itive

It may sometimes be necessary to resort to pharmaceutical medicines to get through the dark times. The rest of the time, though, changing our negative and repetitive thought processes may just require a little more focus, some determination, and the willingness to break lifelong habits that have been hardwired into our brain.

It has been reported that in the early days of the space program, NASA gave astronauts convex goggles that made everything they viewed appear upside down. Can you imagine looking at an upside-down world 24/7? But thirty days later something unexpected happened: the astronauts' brains adapted to this new way of seeing, and their world turned right side up again.[78] Scientists have now determined that it takes the brain a minimum of sixty-six days to begin to create new habits. In approximately two months, and with a strong motivation, old patterns and habits can start to shift as we change the underlying thoughts that fuel them.[79]

I'm not suggesting that we can avoid all negative thoughts that come into our minds. Negative thoughts can be a useful warning signal that we're off course and might want to steer our minds in a more positive direction. For example, you may wonder why you are annoyed by a stranger in a checkout line at the store. If you ignore the thought, you might direct your anger toward your girlfriend later. If instead you take a moment to check in with your thoughts as they are happening, you may realize that the stranger reminds you of a childhood bully and the uncomfortable feelings that memory brings with it. Recognizing the truth that underlies our thinking helps us to begin the process of changing our perceptions and ensuing reactions. Do this for a couple of months, and like the astronauts, you too may find that your world turns right side up again!

Your cat and dog may not be able to help with every bad thought you have, but they can help reduce the charge of your negative thinking and provide you with the space and time that you need to return to better-feeling thoughts, as Sophie did for Karen.

Sophie & Karen

Eight years ago, I went through a difficult period. My husband and I had just moved away from a town that we loved, leaving my friends and my business behind. I was initially excited by the move, but over time I found myself lonely and had trouble adapting to my new surroundings. One day my husband looked at me and said, "You know what you need, Karen? You need a dog."

It was the best idea he's ever had.

Sophie is a shih tzu, and she was the runt of her litter. We brought her home on my birthday and she was a wonderful gift. My husband was not a dog person but Sophie won him over immediately. I loved Sophie from the moment I saw her, but my loneliness proved stronger than my love for her.

I began to experience anxiety attacks that would sometimes last up to three days. At first I was told that I had mercury poisoning and I underwent some treatments. But the anxiety didn't go away. I felt agitated and desperate, and didn't know what to do.

I had never been a big drinker, but when I had the occasional glass of wine it always made me feel better. I got the thought in my head that if a little bit is good, then a lot is better. Before I knew it, I was drinking every day. I would wake up at 2 A.M. and drink; then I'd wake up in the morning and drink some more.

During this time, Sophie would come up to me, smell my breath, and then back up with disgust. It was as if she was saying, "You are not the person who came and got me. You are different, and I don't like it."

Things finally got so bad that I ended up in rehab, and eventually in Alcoholics Anonymous. About twenty months ago I stopped drinking completely, and it was then that my relationship with Sophie changed.

Today, our relationship has become one of connection. Instead of trying to move away from me, Sophie practically does backflips when I get home. When I ask her for a kiss, she eagerly gives me one. I talk to her and tell her how much I treasure her and how much she enriches my life. And she looks back at me with her little face, as if to say, "I understand, tell me more!"

Being sober is an evolving process. It doesn't end with you no longer taking a drink. Sobriety is about unraveling the layers of yourself and getting a better understanding of who you are. Every once in a while I think it would be great to have a glass of wine, but then I look at Sophie and see the love she has for me and I tell myself, "No, you can't do that; enjoy your good life, don't go back, keep moving ahead." These are the new thoughts that fill my mind now.

In AA they teach us that it's important to make amends to those we have hurt with our addiction. In my case, it wasn't just people, like my husband and friends, that I injured through my behavior. I had hurt Sophie too, and I felt guilty for what I put her through. So, while I was sitting on the couch with her one night, I decided to make amends to her.

"Sophie," I said out loud, "what happened wasn't good, and I wasn't the best mom for you during that time. I'm sorry, I love you, and from this moment on we are going forward . . . together."

It felt good to say that to her, and I do feel that she has forgiven me. Unlike people, dogs understand that no human is perfect. My husband and I never had children, and while I don't mistake Sophie for a child, I do think she is as happy as we are. Sophie's taught me that you can make the best of anything, and that any day can be a good day as long as we have each other. With her beside me, my life feels more complete.

Paws for your Prescription!

From the office of
Nurse Kitty Wiskas and Dr. Harry Friend

1. Notice your thoughts. Do you tend to see the world as the cat bowl half empty or half full?

2. Distraction in action, remembering our superpowers, groovin' by movin', creating a happy list, and thinking *pawsitive* are all things that can help you enjoy your life even more.

3. Negative thoughts are not the bad guys. Like alarms, they alert you to pay attention. Learn to listen, let them go as soon as you can, and then come outside and enjoy a nap in the sunshine with us!

COMING UP: You are becoming keenly aware of how powerful your thoughts are. But did you know there's also power in how you choose to verbalize them? Read on!

CHAPTER 11

The Impact of Words

"A cat is more intelligent than people believe,
and can be taught any crime."

—Ralph Waldo Emerson

When you feel on top of the world, you might say, "I feel amazing!" If instead you wake up with the blues, you might say, "I'm depressed." You may think these are just words, but take notice of how you feel when you say "amazing or depressed" to yourself out loud. For most people, saying the positive words feels infinitely better than saying the negative ones. Research shows that 75 to 90 percent of all visits to primary care physicians are for stress-related problems. Stress affecting children, teenagers, and the elderly has also risen.[80] Our emotional reactions to our stress and the words we use to describe those emotions are important for us to be aware of.

According to Andrew Newber, MD and Mark Robert Waldman, coauthors of *Words Can Change your Brain*, a single positive word—like "peace" or "love"—can alter the expression of our genes and make us more resilient. Hostile language, in contrast, can interfere with genes that play a key role in protecting us from stress.[81]

Dr. Masaru Emoto's book *The Hidden Messages in Water* contains photographs of ice crystals taken under a microscope. The water in the ice crystals that were exposed to loving words (joy, gratitude, wisdom) or beautiful music show brilliant snowflake patterns. In contrast, the water that was exposed to negative words ("you make me sick," "I hate you," etc.) and heavy metal music formed distorted patterns.[82] You can see the images of these crystals on my online photo gallery: www.Animal HumanHealth.com/gallery/

The images of the crystals are stunning, but do we really need them to prove that a mind filled with gratitude, hope, and compassion is healthier than one stuck in a loop of despair, irritability, or judgment?

Our emotions add dimension to our life; they help us empathize with others and are an expression of our humanity. To feel the spectrum of human emotion from fear to love is normal and unavoidable. But wouldn't it be nice not to be stuck in the lower emotions for any longer than necessary? Wouldn't our quality of life improve if we woke up to appreciation, rather than anxiety? What if we could go through life with the belief that we are of value for no other reason than just because we exist?

Of all of the people to whom I've asked the question, "If your dog were your doctor or your cat your nurse, what advice would they give you?" not one dog lover has responded, "My dog would advise me to be angrier and to worry more." Not one cat guardian has said, "My cat really inspires me to be less patient and act more selfishly." In fact, they've said quite the opposite, sharing tales of love, connection, and gratitude that have touched their hearts, enriched their lives, and served as a source of joy.

I've seen my cats and dogs feel sadness at the passing of one of our pack. I've seen Rudy grow aggressive when he doesn't like another dog. Dakota might even get jealous from time to time. The difference is, I don't see my companions staying in that space for any extended length of time. Animals have an uncanny ability to release the past and live in the moment—sometimes even when they've lived through cruel and unimaginable experiences. Animals teach us, inspire us, and gently nudge us to leave the rotting fruits of intolerance, arrogance, and anger at the bottom of our emotional trees and instead to reach for trust, joy, and love, the ripe fruits that hang off the higher branches.

If a dog were your therapist or a cat your counselor, what words of wisdom would they offer you? The following nine stories reveal how cats and dogs have helped their guardians through many of life's challenges. From surviving a life-threatening illness to learning self-acceptance to recognizing the importance of freedom, our animal friends continue to inspire us towards a healthier, happier, and more extraordinary life.

Awareness: Marley & Jacob

My dog Jasper died of cancer. He was a Great Pyrenees, and the epitome of everything I had always wanted in a dog. When he died, it crushed me to such a degree that after five years I am still having a hard time with his loss.

After Jasper died, my wife was so sad that two weeks later she rescued two dogs, Marley and Chester, from the shelter, hoping they would help us heal. But I wasn't ready for another dog and didn't want them in our home. My heart was broken, and I felt resentful that they were here and my Great Pyrenees was not. I couldn't give these dogs the love they needed, and that was also hard because that wasn't me . . . I love animals.

One day, we were at the beach playing tag with my son William, who was five years old at the time. He would run up to the waves and when they got close he would run away from them. William was having a great time, but the more he laughed and squealed, the more Marley paced back and forth agitatedly. It was clear to me that he was uncomfortable with William being near the waves. I think he sensed there was danger. Finally, Marley ran up to William, grabbed him by the back of his pants, and pulled him back up to the beach.

In that moment, I realized that there was something special happening. What if this had been in traffic? Or what if there was a sneaker wave? Marley was looking out for William. He was protecting him.

As I stood there watching, something clicked inside of me. I realized there was something going on here that was bigger than me and my little world and the trauma of loss I had experienced when Jasper died. Marley was showing me that he was looking out for my family. This little dog made me come face to face with the fact that my hang-ups were my hang-ups, and not his. I needed to move on with my life, and part of moving on was accepting Marley and Chester into our lives.

Marley and Chester's influence has helped me realize that everyone deserves a second chance. That day on the beach was life-changing for me. It brought me to a new awareness, and for that I am grateful.

Gratitude: Boomer & Cynthia

At 2:30 A.M. I woke up to my dog, Boomer, barking uncontrollably. I assumed a raccoon or possum was outside, but when Boomer wouldn't stop, I got out of bed and went downstairs. Boomer was sniffing, scratching, and snarling at the front door—a very different reaction than when he barks at people who leave business cards there. I tried to calm him down but he ignored me and continued barking furiously.

Boomer is a ten-year old Catahoula leopard mix who I rescued many years ago from a shelter where I used to volunteer. His right front leg had been broken and hadn't been properly attended to, so it jutted out, causing him to limp. He also had a hip injury that affected his mobility. But Boomer's injuries have never slowed him down or dampened his spirit. Even with his rickety legs, he is still a protective companion.

As Boomer continue to snarl at the door, I peeked through the window and saw that there was a man standing on the other side. He was tall and wearing a baseball cap, and he was keeping his head down so I couldn't see his face. At first I thought it was my son's friend's father, Tony. I called out to him—but he didn't respond. So I grabbed the phone and called my son's friend's mother to ask why Tony was at our front door. She told me Tony was out of town, so it couldn't be him.

I was nervous, but with Boomer beside me, I didn't feel afraid. We climbed the stairs to take a better look from the balcony. From this vantage point I could see that the man was trying to put a key into the door to unlock it. When he looked up, I saw that he was a complete stranger, and he was clearly drunk. Eventually Boomer's commanding bark and my insistence that he leave drove the man away.

Courage may come naturally to dogs, but it's what came after Boomer's warning that really touched me. After the man left, Boomer kept jumping on me, trying to get me to play with him. It was as if he could sense that I had been shaken and was trying to get me to let go of what had just happened. I also believe that Boomer truly felt useful and needed, like he had done his job. He seemed proud of himself, and I was proud of him too.

Before this incident, Boomer slept on the sofa, but now he sleeps on his bed on the floor next to me and doesn't leave my side. Periodically he will get up for a reassuring pat, but it feels like it's more for me than for him—as if he's concerned and wants me to feel safe. What's even sweeter is that Nina, who is the dominant dog in our house, is treating Boomer like a king! What a great, magical, and courageous dog Boomer is. I feel lucky and grateful to have him in our lives.

Commitment: Josie, Jezebel, Stephen & Tanya

When I first started dating Stephen, I was living with two cats, Josie and Jezebel, who I had adopted a couple of years earlier. Jezebel was a black-and-white cat with markings around her mouth that looked like a mustache and a goatee and reminded me of Charlie Chaplin. Josie, meanwhile, had white, lima bean–shaped spots on her body that made her look a little bit like a cow.

Stephen worked in the financial world and dressed very well. I found lots to love about him, especially his confidence and sense of humor. As time went on, things began to grow serious between us. One day, he said to me, "If we're going to get engaged and marry, you are really going to have to think about doing something with those two cats."

I was stunned. "What do you mean?"

"Well, they get cat hair all over my suits, and I can't have that for work. Besides, I'm not really a cat person, Tanya."

Wow! I thought to myself. What I said was, "You knew I had cats when we first started dating."

Stephen listened and said nothing.

"I am not getting rid of my cats," I went on. "If you want to date me, if you want to get engaged, and if you want to marry me, then it's a package deal. Maybe you should date someone who doesn't have cats."

The air filled with an uncomfortable silence. I didn't know if Stephen would stay or go. I really liked him and wanted us to stay together, but I knew that I wasn't getting rid of my cats no matter what.

We continued dating and never spoke of it again.

One night Stephen came over for dinner. He had slipped off his shoes so he could be comfortable, and he was in his stocking feet. As we ate, I spotted Josie under the table, and I realized that Stephen was gently stroking her back with his foot. He was doing this so subtly, thinking that I wouldn't realize he was doing it at all.

I played along as if I didn't know this interaction was happening, but in that moment I knew my cats had won Stephen over and everything was going to be fine.

Stephen and I did get married, and since then he has become one of the best animal guardians I have ever seen. He takes the care of our animal companions VERY seriously, and he spares no expense when it comes to their well-being.

When Josie and Jezebel grew old and it was their time to go, Stephen was heartbroken; and when they passed away, he cried as much as I did. It was a great surprise to me to see how hard he took the loss.

There are two things I learned from this situation: One, stick to your guns when it comes to your animals, because they are family, and when you make that commitment, it's for life. And two, don't judge someone too harshly who may feel differently than you about animals. If you stand your ground quietly and firmly, you may help them unlock all of the love they are afraid to show. We're always evolving, and sometimes people need a little more time to get to a place of greater compassion. But be patient; they can get there.

Joy: Finn & Danny

I've had dogs my whole life, but when I got sick with liver cancer, I didn't have one. I'm a Vietnam vet, and during my chemotherapy at the Veterans Hospital, I knew it wasn't looking good for me; at best, I was going to be ill for a long while. I figured if I was going to be sick I wanted a dog to keep me company.

I decided that the ideal dog to adopt would be old, long-haired, about 100 pounds, and would enjoy lazing around in bed with me. So I went to the Marin Humane Society and told them exactly who I was looking for. They brought me back to look at the available dogs. But instead of finding a huge old dog, a three-month-old, four-inch-tall mouse of a dog walked right up to me. He looked me straight in the face, and I took one look at him and said out loud, "That's my dog!"

Everyone laughed, because I'm 6'7"and my shoes were bigger than this little dog was, but I didn't care. Finn picked me, and I instantly fell in love with him.

Our next stop was the pet store, where I bought my new pug-dachs-hund-terrier-Chihuahua $500 worth of toys. He was so happy, and I've never been so in love in my life.

During the time I was sick with cancer, Finn was my doctor, my nurse, and my companion. He also was my empath. He knew exactly how I felt, what I needed in the moment, and what was best for me. When I got really sick and felt nauseous and weak, he would just lie there and watch me. When I felt better, he would play with me. When I got tired, he would put his head under my chin and we would both go to sleep. I was pretty sick for about a year, but Finn was there for me through it all until I got well again.

Now that I've recovered, we go horseback riding together. Finn's too little to walk beside the horses, so I put him in my saddlebag. Finny sits in the bag with his head poking out and people laugh because it looks like I'm riding around with a squirrel.

Animals give you unconditional friendship and joy. No matter how you feel, whether happy, mad, sad, or frustrated, they just sit there with a face full of joy looking back at you. It's so healing.

Finn's companionship has meant the world to me during one of the most challenging times of my life. Joy—this is the gift this little mouse of a dog has given me.

Trust: Gracie & Sandie

Nine years ago, my friend Lisa and I were driving through an undeveloped area when she said, "Hey, I think I just saw a kitten."

"Keep driving," I told her.

She looked at me. "Did you really just say that?"

I laughed. "Of course I didn't, let's go back and find her."

At this point, we had been rescuing cats and caring for them for several years. Over the next three days we set up a trap and captured five five-week-old kittens and one five-month-old grey tabby with incredible green eyes that I named Gracie.

The babies were easy to adopt out, but I couldn't find a home for Gracie because she was feral and wary of humans. I decided I would spay her, then release her back outside when she was healthy again.

After her operation, I brought Gracie home and set her up in my walk-in closet so she could convalesce in a quiet and secure spot. The problem was that Lisa and I were in the process of moving, and if I was going to release Gracie, I didn't know who in the area would take on the responsibility of feeding her. Feral cats may seem wild but they often still depend on people for food. I was racking my brain—did I know someone with property who could feed her? Or maybe someone with a big backyard? No one came to mind.

Though she was getting better each day from her spaying, Gracie wasn't coming out of the back of my closet. I would approach her and talk to her, and when I would try to touch her she wouldn't hiss or bite me, but it was clear that she didn't want to have anything to do with me, either.

As I began to spend more time in the closet with Gracie, though, something began to change. A trust began to build up between us. On the third week, I touched Gracie and to my surprise she bent into my hand and started purring. I started crying, and Gracie purred even more.

Gracie had never trusted a human before, and the joy of having her trust me felt like an honor. I had finally found Gracie her forever home . . . with me. Gracie slept in my bed that night, and has done so every night for the nine years since. She loves to sleep under the covers and even eats ice cream with me.

Gracie inspired me to start my Kittens and Cattens Rescue, which I have set up in the back of my pet food store, The Pet Cottage, in San Anselmo, California. To date we have adopted well over seven hundred cats and kittens to their forever homes, and our organization is going strong. I have Gracie to thank for that.

Recently Gracie began to lose weight, and after a trip to our vet we found out she has feline leukemia. The vet gave her six weeks to live; that was six months ago. Still, Gracie has been getting skinnier and skinnier, and she will probably be leaving us in the next few days.

What has Gracie taught me? Trust. Gracie trusted me when she had no reason to. She didn't know me from Adam, but still she got in the trap we set for her, and once we caught her she didn't struggle to get out. In fact, she didn't even panic when I put her in my closet. Gracie trusted me from the beginning, and on the third week she stepped through the invisible wall that kept us apart. We bonded in an instant, and we've been best friends ever since.

Most people won't adopt a cat with leukemia, but Gracie lived nine years without any symptoms. Mattie, our current shop cat, also has feline leukemia, but because of Gracie I now trust that people can care for a cat with this disease and that they can have a good quality of life together.

Recently, Gracie started sleeping on a chair near my two dogs. She has never done that before. Even now, her trust keeps growing. She trusts that I will do the right thing by her, and let her go when the time is right. Gracie's time is coming to an end . . . but it's not over. Not just yet.

Inspiration: Autumn & Stephanie

My friend is an Animal Control officer in New Jersey. While on her beat, she was called to a puppy mill, where dogs were being bred in overcrowded, filthy, and deplorable conditions. While she was there, she rescued a five-month-old dachshund and asked if I would take the puppy for a while until she could find her a permanent home. I agreed—but it didn't take long for that little puppy to work her way into my heart. I named her Autumn because her fur reminded me of the color of the leaves as they turn in the fall.

Shortly after her sixth birthday, Autumn woke up shivering and shaking. Her gait was wobbly, her stomach was distended, and she was in tremendous pain. Suddenly her back-end collapsed, and she lost control of both her bowels and bladder. I rushed her to the emergency clinic, where doctors told me she was suffering from intervertebral disc disease (IVDD) and needed surgery to remove a ruptured disc in her back.

One week and ten thousand dollars later, the clinic gave me my dog back and told me she had a less than 5 percent chance of mobility or hope for any quality of life.

"Look Stephanie," the vet said, "she can't urinate on her own, she can't hold in her bowel movements, she can't walk, she can't this, and she can't that . . ."

"Well what can she do?" I interrupted. The way I saw it, Autumn was alive, and no longer in pain. "Can she live with this condition?" I asked.

"Well . . . yes."

"Then show me how to take care of her."

When they told me not to waste my money or time on rehab, I found another vet.

For the next few months, Autumn went through rehab that included acupuncture and nutrition. I learned how to express her bladder and bowels (which, I was surprised to find, hardly took any time at all—only about four seconds), and she got fitted for a cart so she could get around on her own. Initially, Autumn couldn't feel her hind legs, but within six months, she started to walk reflexively on her own.

These days, Autumn lives a happy and comfortable life. She never has accidents, her bed is nice and clean, and she sleeps through the night without a problem. Every day, she gets into her little cart and she and Chip, my other dachshund, and I go on our half-mile walk together. When Autumn was in the hospital, she wouldn't eat unless Chip came in to visit. He's like a big brother to her. When she was sick he would sit with her. His support and love helped Autumn bounce back.

Everyone in our neighborhood knows Autumn. Kids come up and want to hear her story to understand why she uses the cart. Autumn even has her own Facebook page, "Autumn The IVDD Dachshund," where we post helpful hints for others living with this condition. Pet parents who lack a solid and well-versed medical team often don't realize there are other options besides euthanasia. And that's sad, because, as Autumn shows us, IVDD dogs are healthy pups who simply need a little extra TLC.

Autumn inspires me in so many ways. After everything that has happened to her, she hasn't missed a beat. She may only have two legs instead of four, but that doesn't stop her spirit. Autumn has taught me that it doesn't matter what life throws at you; if you deal with the hand that you're dealt and keep moving forward, you'll be okay.

Because of Autumn I'm more understanding of other people's challenges. I realize that everybody is going through something, and that I sometimes need to be more patient, considerate, and loving.

Please never give up on your dog, because they will never give up on you. Love them the way they would love you. Think about that when you look at them—that no matter what kind of day you've had, they're always there for you, always happy to see you. They all deserve a chance. Autumn's story inspires me. I hope it does the same for you.

Self-Acceptance: Puddycat & Diane

When I was a little girl, I desperately wanted a horse. When I was nine, my folks told me that if I saved enough money they would match what I had and I could buy one. So for months I washed cars, weeded yards, and saved every penny of my birthday money and allowance.

Finally, when I was eleven, I had earned enough money. Rio was the horse of my dreams—a pure white quarter horse and Arabian mix with the sweetest blue eyes. I spent all of my time with him, brushing him or just hanging out in his barn for hours. After school, I'd take him into the forest and ride him bareback through the woods—quite the adventure for an eleven-year-old girl. Some days I'd sing to him and he'd rest his head on my shoulder and close his eyes until his head would be so heavy I'd buckle under his weight.

For a year and a half Rio and I were best friends. I felt like I was in heaven, and had the most wonderful life anyone could imagine. Then that life changed. My father, who was in the Coast Guard, was transferred to Anchorage, Alaska. I had to leave behind a place I loved, my friends, and most importantly, my beloved horse.

Life in Anchorage couldn't have been more different—or difficult. We arrived in the dead of winter, when everything as far as the eye could see was frozen. At 65 degrees below zero with a 40 mile-per-hour wind chill factor, Anchorage felt like another planet. The day we got there, a woman ran into our lodge screaming at the top of her lungs because her fingers had gotten frostbitten.

Forty years ago, Anchorage was a small town. All of the local kids had grown up together since kindergarten, and they had absolutely no interest in an outsider like me. I would make efforts to reach out to them, but they never reached back. I felt rejected, and eventually developed the attitude that if they didn't want to have anything to do with me then I didn't want to have anything to do with them, either.

My parents didn't understand what I was going through. I started talking back to them and acting out my frustrations because I felt sad and lonely. My mother, who had grown up in the Netherlands during a time when kids were seen and not heard, was especially intolerant of my behavior. I was constantly at odds with her, and over time, I grew angrier and more withdrawn.

My isolation became depression. I would find myself in bed until noon, unable to face the world. My depression became so bad that I began thinking of ways to end my life. I told myself that I didn't care what other people thought but the truth is, I really did care. I probably would have ended my life if it were not for an unexpected friend.

Puddycat was a black-and-white tuxedo cat that we'd brought with us from Edmonton. She wasn't very cuddly with other people, but she would allow me to hold her, and we slept together at night. Puddycat seemed to be the one being in the whole world who did not reject me. Instead, she accepted me without judgment. Her companionship helped me understand the goodness that all animals inherently have. Because of her unconditional love, I found the acceptance I needed and I chose to go on living.

Puddycat helped me get through the dark and lonely time of my adolescence, and she helped me realize the amazing beings that animals are. She died when she was sixteen, but she continues to have an influence on my work today. Because of her inspiration and unconditional acceptance, I am an animal advocate with a passion and commitment to help all animals. And I even host a radio show on animal welfare and advocacy in Southern Oregon.

If Puddycat were my nurse, she would tell me not to be so concerned with the acceptance of others but instead to accept myself, as she so easily accepted me. Kindness, love, and above all self-acceptance, this is what Puddycat taught me.

Hope: Bella & Peter

Many years ago, I was diagnosed with severe depression. I was thrown into a room with a plastic-covered mattress on the floor and held there for seventy-two hours.

Today I am the Chairman of the Board for the United States Psychiatric Rehabilitation Association, now known as the Psychiatric Rehabilitation Association, and my mission in life is to work toward changing the system so that no one else has to go through the experience I went through. I continue to live with depression, but I've learned how to manage my symptoms by taking good care of myself and maintaining a support system of friends and peers. Bella, my eleven-year old brindle shih tzu and psychiatric service dog, has also been vital to my recovery.

Bella helps me in many ways. Because she needs me to feed her, care for her, and walk her three times a day, she is the motivator I need to get out and face the world. Bella keeps me from isolating myself, succumbing to depression, and becoming idle.

No matter how busy I get with work, Bella also reminds me to take my medication twice a day. She goes over to the pill boxes and barks at them. Once she knows I've picked them up, she stops barking.

I do a tremendous amount of traveling, so I rely on sleep medication to keep my sleeping schedule normal. If a fire alarm were to go off, Bella would jump on my chest until I wake up—otherwise, I would likely sleep through the alarm.

Recently, I was sitting on a couch next to Bella when the fire alarm went off. Bella started pacing, wondering how she was going to get me on the floor and jump on my chest. I picked her up and held her to me, letting her know that everything was going to be okay and that we could move on from here.

Bella can also read my anxiety even when I can't. Once I was New Mexico for work and unexpectedly found myself speaking to TV, newspaper, and radio reporters. I'd had no time to prepare for this, and while I stood at the podium, talking and answering questions, I began to grow anxious. Bella sat in her chair in the audience, watching me. She has been trained to

always stay in her seat when I'm speaking in front of an audience, no mat-
ter what—and she obeyed that training. But when my anxiety began to go
through the roof, she stood up in a full point posture and would not break
eye contact with me. This was her cue to me that I needed to do something
about my anxiety. As my levels of anxiety continued to elevate, her cues grew
more and more intense.

When the cameras stopped rolling and I moved away from the podium,
Bella leaped into my arms. To ease my anxiety, I began to gently stroke
her, and immediately my heart rate and anxiety quieted, and I started to
breathe more calmly.

There is a bond between me and Bella that is unstoppable. We know how
to read each other. Her eyes let me know when she's thirsty and needs water,
and I can talk things out with her that I would normally keep inside of myself.
Just having her listen is enough for me to figure out the solution to a problem
that I might be having. Bella helps me get through even the darkest times.

A friend of mine recently lost her dog, and it drove me into a very diffi-
cult space where I was thinking, What in god's name would I do if anything
ever happened to Bella?

So I volunteered at a shih tzu center here in the area and was intro-
duced to Athos, who has since come to live with me and Bella. Athos is
the gentlest dog you could ever imagine, and together, the three of us have
become the Three Musketeers.

Bella helps me fulfill the passion I feel for changing a system so that
it offers better services to others who are suffering from clinical depression
and other mental illnesses. For those of us who suffer from this illness, it's all
about getting through the night and into the next day so we don't succumb
to our demons. Bella helps me get through the tough spots and offers me
hope. She has given me back my dignity.

Freedom: Chance & Michelle

When I was in college, I worked at the Berkeley Humane Society. I would
open up in the morning, clean out stalls during the day, and close up the
facility at night. I hadn't thought to adopt a dog, but when I saw Chance, I

completely fell for him. I have no idea what he had been through before, but since he landed in the shelter, I was sure it hadn't been an easy time for him.

When Chance was neutered, I was there during the surgery. I even lifted his leg during the procedure. After the operation he tried to walk over to me, but he was so groggy that he could barely lift his head. Chance is a large husky-shepherd mix, and he is pretty independent. But I sensed that he didn't want to be left alone. Every night I stayed an hour past the end of my shift just to sit in his kennel and be with him. I loved him from the start, and I decided that I was going to do whatever it took to adopt this dog and give him a happy life.

When I came home for summer vacation, my parents told me that Chance could not live with us. I have always been a huge animal lover, but my parents did not grow up in an animal-friendly home. Because they didn't have this exposure to animals, they didn't know that animals have feelings, or that they are gentle, loving, and kind. So Chance and I went to live with my aunt through the summer and until school started again.

Over those few months, even though Chance wasn't living in their home, my parents were exposed to all of the wonderful attributes dogs have; qualities that they had never realized. For example, when my mom was sad and no one else seemed to notice, Chance would come up to her and lay his head on her lap.

"I can't believe he's so perceptive!" she would say. His caring would make her smile and she would begin to feel better again.

That summer totally turned my parents' attitude around. Now my mom loves animals and welcomes them into her home. Even my dad, who used to throw rocks at cats and had no empathy for animals, will take Chance for long walks or go biking with him.

When I got back to school, I found an apartment off campus where Chance and I could live together. I couldn't afford to pay for heat, and it was really cold in Ohio during the winter. One night Chance and I were on the floor in front of my little space heater, trying to stay warm. I had my laptop open and I was watching a video of Chinese fur farms. The video showed dogs pacing nervously in their cages right before they were electrocuted so their fur could be used for garments.

I knew this was going on in the world, but the images hit me hard. I sobbed like a waterfall and couldn't stop. The more I cried, the more Chance kept nudging closer to me. Finally he laid his head on my lap and looked up at me with his big eyes. I was so grateful to have him beside me that night. Those poor dogs would never be free, but Chance was one individual animal that was experiencing freedom. That thought inspired me to work so that every animal could have that same freedom.

Today, I'm an animal advocate and activist. I use video, photography, and social media to inspire and empower people towards more compassionate food and living choices so that animals don't have to suffer. Having Chance by my side reminds me that all animals deserve to be free, to experience joy, and live out their lives as they are meant to. Chance's love inspires me to go further and work harder and more passionately, while at the same time he reminds me to enjoy life, be grateful, and work on my own kind of freedom—from stress. Chance teaches me to focus on what really matters.

Paws for your Prescription!

From the office of
Nurse Kitty Wiskas and Dr. Harry Friend

1. *Joy*, *trust*, and *hope* are animal-inspired words to live by. If you're having trouble coming up with a word to take the place of *sad*, *lonely*, *anxious*, etc., look to us—we're generally modeling a good word at all times!

2. If you're feeling blue, don't ignore how you feel. We're here for you when you're sad, and we will be here when you're ready to smile again.

3. What is your story with your own animal friends? Is it a *tail* about four-legged friendship, the power in playfulness, or finding forgiveness? Share it with Carlyn by going to: AnimalHumanHealth.com/shareyourstory/. You and your animal companion may just end up in her next book!

COMING UP: Perhaps you didn't think you could overcome your thoughts or that animals could add to your positive vocabulary, but hopefully you're beginning to see another way. Ready to go deeper? Let's talk about how your body speaks!

CHAPTER 12

How Your Body Speaks

"Dogs are mirrors that bark."

—Michael McCullough, LAc

After many years of treating patients with an array of health issues, it has become clear to me that most people are unaware that their aches, pains, and illnesses serve any purpose other than to make them suffer. Although my patients are treating their symptoms in a natural way, with acupuncture and nutrition, I know that unless their deeper issues are addressed (such as underlying stresses, emotional layers, and even issues of the spirit), their bodies will likely produce another symptom or illness to make their message heard.

For this reason, at the beginning of my treatments, and before I insert the first needle, I ask my patients to take a moment to check in with themselves and let me know in their own words what their body is saying to them.

The body speaks, though usually through physical sensations rather than words. Tingling, tightness, aches, pain, and even temperature fluctuations can be ways that our body might nudge us toward looking at something deeper about ourselves. Our body also speaks through emotions, like fear, sadness, and grief. Sometimes a forgotten memory will accompany these emotions.

During a motivational seminar, Jack Canfield, co-creator of the #1 *New York Times* best-selling series *Chicken Soup for the Soul®* and the author of *The Success Principles,* explained that many of us feel frustrated and unable to create the lives that we want because we have a six-year-old version of ourselves running the show. Many of our limiting beliefs are formed when we are children. These beliefs affect our ability to get the jobs we want, the relationships we desire, and the happiness we wish we had.

During the seminar, Jack led the audience through a body-scan exercise and asked us to become present to the sensations and feelings we were experiencing. He shared that when he first did this exercise he felt a huge band of tension across the back of his shoulders. As he tuned into the feeling, he began to remember a decision he had made as a young child—one that went on to define who he became as an adult:

> I was abused as a child. My dad was an alcoholic and used to beat me when he was drunk. I would hide from him wherever I could. Remember those old radio consoles that contained a tiny radio and big speakers? If my dad was drunk, I used to pull the device over to the wall and hide behind it. I'd wait there for hours without making a sound until my dad went to bed just so I wouldn't get beaten.
>
> Because my dad was so violent, my mom finally divorced him and we went to live with my grandmother. I was six years old and this transitional time was difficult for me.
>
> Fortunately, I had a dog that I really loved. Like the blanket that the Linus character in the Peanuts cartoons carries for security, my dog helped me feel comforted and safe.
>
> One day, my dog bit a neighbor and the dogcatcher came to our house to euthanize him. My dog and I hid together under my grandmother's house while they looked everywhere for us. As we huddled together, I remembered thinking that he was the only being who I felt safe with and now they were going to take him away from me. Eventually the dogcatcher found us. He took my dog and I never saw him again.

A friend of mine says, "Tears are how you water your growth." This childhood experience, as painful as it was, has given me great empathy for people who have been abused. By reliving the experience in a six-year-old body and watching my dog being taken away, I remembered making a decision that I was going to protect the "underdogs" of the world.

After I did the body-scan exercise, I went home and cleared out the "shoulds" in my life. Instead, I began doing what I really wanted to do, which was to make a difference by helping people on a larger scale while at the same time caring for myself. There was a powerful gift in remembering the pain. It made me stronger.

THE FIVE ELEMENTS

Chinese medicine provides a basis for understanding the body's emotional language through a system called the Five Elements. A profound and ancient body of knowledge, the Five Elements explain how everything that exists in the universe can be divided into five aspects of nature: wood, fire, earth, metal, and water. These elements correspond to different organ systems in the body, in particular the liver, heart, spleen, lung, and kidneys. In turn, these organs match up to different human emotions: anger, anxiety, worry, grief, and fear. When these five emotions become excessive or fall out of balance, disease can be the result.

ELEMENT	wood	fire	earth	metal	water
ORGANS	liver	heart	spleen	lung	kidney
EMOTIONS	anger, rage, resentment	anxiety	worry, overthinking	grief	fear

According to Five Element theory, the anger and resentment that may come from seeing others happy and successful when we are not can eventually affect the liver and lead to headaches or even depression. Anxiety over the unknown might result in palpitations or insomnia. Worry and overthinking, often the hallmark of the new college student, might present as digestive disorders. Prolonged fear can affect the kidneys, manifesting in a child wetting their bed. The grief over the loss of a loved one that remains in mourning stage (rather than moving into a celebration of the life they lived) could eventually lead to a respiratory issue such as a chronic cough.

The way your body speaks is not a formula. It's not black and white. But being aware of our inner world allows us to explore the unique ways in which our bodies communicate with us, and the Five Element system gives us a great starting point for that. Ultimately, just like in any successful relationship, the trick is to be willing and courageous enough to listen with an open heart, learn from what is being said, and integrate that information into our lives.

Sometimes we need a little help from our animal friends to help us figure out how to listen to our bodies. Susan, an acupuncturist, discovered this from her dog Trinity after she solved the perplexing case of the mysteriously appearing milk jugs.

Trinity & Susan

I used to live in a house in the Santa Cruz mountains that was surrounded by nature and lots of space where my two dogs, Woofie and Trinity, could roam free. After we'd been there for a while, I began to find plastic milk jugs on our driveway when I came home after work. I couldn't figure out how they were getting there until I arrived home one day and caught Trinity, my ninety-six-pound golden lab/McNab mix, having a wonderful time kicking a jug down our steep driveway like a soccer ball. He had been going to the neighbors' trash bins, digging out the jugs, and bringing them home to play with.

As I watched Trinity kicking those milk jugs around, I was taken by how joyful he looked, and it gave me an inspiration for a tool to recommend to my patients.

I have been a teacher and practitioner of traditional Chinese medicine for over thirty years, and lately I had been treating a lot of people for migraine headaches and TMJ (a disorder of the joint in the jaw that makes it click or pop). I've never met a migraine or TMJ sufferer who wasn't holding on to an underlying element of repressed rage. These are usually people who are unable to express their feelings, say what they think, or give themselves permission to feel what they feel. So I began to suggest to them that they get some cardboard boxes to kick around. Boxes make a nice loud sound but they don't hurt anything or anyone; they're great for releasing pent-up emotions. A lot of people can't make a sound with their voice to express their anger, but they can do it with a cardboard box. Tearing those boxes apart feels very satisfying, and it's a great way to release anger in a private, safe, and healthy way.

If a person is not allowed to say what they feel or be who they are, if life or family members shut them down, it creates congestion in their liver organ system. The liver loves to express itself in creative ways, but it needs to flow freely. When it is not allowed to do so, it shuts down and becomes a powder keg. Women with congested livers can come down with PMS, cramping, and breast pain. Both genders can come down with insomnia and temporal headaches. And when it gets bad enough, congested liver energy can become depression. All sorts of health conditions can result from unexpressed emotions.

I have used the cardboard box–kicking technique often over the years, because Trinity's idea was a good one. But different people have done different things to express their bound-up emotions. I once treated a woman who would go to Goodwill and buy a stack of plates, then smash them all against a brick wall. By the time she was done she would be very happy to spend the next hour cleaning them up. Another patient found relief in lobbing old apples off a cliff with a tennis racket. Yet another liked to rip a phone book in half. All of these activities were different, but all of them helped release some pent-up liver energy.

Trinity demonstrated that bringing awareness to the things we do doesn't have to be complicated; very simple things can get us into very deep places. If your life is not an expression of the beauty of your being, then there is something keeping the lid on that beauty. We are meant to be beings of light, beings of love, and beings of joy. If life is not going in that direction for you, don't settle. Fix it. Like Trinity, find your joy.

DOG AS MY THERAPIST, CAT AS MY COUNSELOR

According to Harvard University, animals can read us. Studies they've conducted show that dogs are superior to chimps and wolves at reading human gestures.[83] But is a dog or a cat's ability to read our cues limited to external signals? Can they go as far as to feel our internal emotions? Can they decipher how our body speaks even when we can't?

If you suffer from IDS—Ignore, Deny, Suppress—you may not always be aware of what you feel, much less have a deeper sense of how your body is speaking to you. Wouldn't it be amazing if your cat or dog, whom you love and trust, could guide you toward a greater understanding of yourself?

Kevin Behan, author of *Your Dog is Your Mirror*, asserts that a dog's behavior is driven by *our* emotions. Dogs don't respond to their human companions based on what they think or do, he says, but rather on what they *feel*. And because of this empathetic ability, dogs can help people connect with their own emotions.[84]

When a dog feels anxious and depressed, mainstream medicine will often turn to prescription drugs. But, instead of numbing a dog because he is feeling fearful or acting out in a way that we don't understand, perhaps we can achieve something greater for our animals by looking for the solution within our own selves.

Just like dogs, cats can be adversely affected by changes in their external environment, like moving to a new home, adding a new family member, or even rearranging the furniture. They can also sense and pick up on our emotions even before we do.

An article in *Animal Wellness Magazine* explains, "Cats and their humans often mirror each other's physical and emotional states. Felines are sensitive creatures, and they can easily take on their human's problems. Because of the bond shared between cats and their families, energetic imbalances may also be shared, and illness can result."[85]

My family found this out the hard way. When we first moved to Northern California and added Teddy the chow to our pack, both Cody and Jester went on strike. They also developed urinary tract infections. Jester got so sick he had to undergo a perineal urethrostomy—a surgery to prevent him from further blockages.

I could say that the move to a new house and the addition of another dog was stressful for the cats, and that would be true. But what is also true is that there were other internal human stressors at play. As much as Ken and I looked forward to our new life together, we were also going through a financial maelstrom that kept us awake at night feeling stressed and anxious. We'd bought a new home thinking that selling our previous home would cover the cost, but it was the year that the housing market dropped, and instead we found ourselves weighed down by two mortgages to pay. To fuel the fire, in moving to Marin County, an area where I had zero patients, I had forfeited my income from my private practice in Los Angeles. To pay for the escalating costs, Ken stayed behind in Los Angeles to work, while I moved up north with Gina, who was starting school.

The separation was hard, but fortunately not permanent. Eventually our house did sell—for much less than we had thought it would, but still, we were free, and Ken was able to move up north and finally be with us. And—surprise! As our internal stresses faded, our cats' stress faded as well. Cody and Jester not only got healthy again, they also became friends with Teddy (though licking a hairy chow often left them hacking up huge black fur balls).

THE MIRROR HAS SIX FACES

Knowing that my cats and dogs reflect something deeper about me makes it pretty hard for me to run away from myself—especially since at one point, my mirror had six different faces. Every one of my cats and dogs has shown me something unique about myself. Sometimes they are good things, and sometimes they are parts of my personality that could use a little work. Roxy reflected my strength, but she also reminded me to work on being more vulnerable. With Teddy, I saw my aloofness and how I set myself apart from others, but he also reminded me that I have a great sense of loyalty. Jester was the most forgiving creature I've ever met, and he reminded me that often I am not—especially toward myself. Dakota shows me my softer, more playful side and encourages me to work on one of my greatest challenges in this lifetime: patience. Cody forced me to admit that I have a grumpy side, and together we worked on letting that go, especially first thing in the morning. Rudy reflects the part of me that wants to do things perfectly, gets frustrated when I don't, and needs to be reminded that there is no "perfect"—that doing the best that I can is enough.

Tonight, as you are sitting on the couch and watching a TV show you may have already seen before, take a moment to tune into your animal friends instead. Think of a behavior or quality they may have that annoys you, or, instead, one that you enjoy. Next, pull out an imaginary mirror and consider what their behavior may be reflecting back at you. The better we know ourselves, the more we will grow, and ultimately, the happier we *and our dogs and cats* can become.

Paws for your Prescription!

From the office of
Nurse Kitty Wiskas and Dr. Harry Friend

1. Emotions are not the bad guys. Don't shut them off. When your body speaks, listen!

2. You ignored the knots in your neck even though we repeatedly tried to get you off the computer by lying across the keyboard. Now you are getting headaches and yelling at us too. Please take better care of yourself so we can all be healthier and happier.

3. Which of the five elements do you need help balancing? Maybe it's time to visit your friendly acupuncturist. And when you do, take us with you; we love acupuncture too!

COMING UP: How high is your EQ? If you thought I meant to say "IQ" . . . read the next pages slowly.

CHAPTER 13

The Value of Emotional Intelligence

"A cat has absolute emotional honesty: human beings, for one reason or another, may hide their feelings, but a cat does not."

—Earnest Hemingway

There are IQ tests to measure how smart we are, but did you know that there are EQ tests that measure your ability to manage your emotions? "EQ" stands for "emotional quotient" (i.e., emotional intelligence), and people who get high scores on these tests tend to deal better with conflicts, maintain better relationships, and be more empathetic toward others.

There was a time when IQ was our measure of success, but according to Daniel Goleman, Pulitzer prize–winner and author, "People who possess high emotional intelligence are the people who truly succeed in work as well as play, building flourishing careers and lasting, meaningful relationships."[86]

How much happier would you be if you were comfortable expressing your emotions, regardless of what anyone else thinks? Would you have a greater sense of freedom if you felt confident enough to go up and talk to someone you've never met before? How much better would your life become if you felt comfortable even when facing unpleasant challenges?

Having a higher EQ can improve the quality of your life by helping you avoid negative self-talk and self-defeating behaviors like smoking, binge eating, or excessive drinking. Developing a better EQ can help you manage your emotions with greater insight and grace; it is a way to become more resilient in these demanding times.

Our dogs may not have the IQ of Albert Einstein, or our cats that of Madame Curie; they can't balance our checkbooks or help us run our businesses; but they do know how to touch our hearts, offer us comfort, and help us turn our tears into smiles. Search your memory for the moments of emotional connection that you have shared with your animal companions in the past. What gifts have they given you through their unconditional love? The more we cultivate our connections to our cats and dogs, the more they can help us enhance our emotional intelligence and improve the quality of our lives.

5 WAYS YOUR CATS & DOGS CAN INCREASE YOUR EQ

1. Yawn More, Bark Less

Did you know that dogs yawn five times more often when they see or hear a human they know yawning? Studies suggest that this type of yawning is related to empathy.[87] Empathy is a key element of emotional intelligence. Being empathetic allows us connect better with others and leads to more meaningful relationships. We don't know if dog yawning replicates human empathy exactly, but the next time your cats or dogs yawn, it's a good opportunity to remember the mirror principle and check your own emotional gauge to see how you are feeling. You may find that there is more to their yawn than meets the eye.

2. Don't Take Yourself So Seriously

A friend of mine gifted me a book called *Walter the Farting Dog*. Even the title made me laugh, because (as all you dog lovers out there know) it's a fact of life: when dogs fart, humans laugh. Dogs don't understand *why* we're laughing at something so natural, but they do love to see us happy. Cats are more regal and not amused by such lowly displays; they prefer to melt away your seriousness by purring you to sleep. Luckily, either approach works.

3. Let the Wind Blow Back Your Ears

We humans tend to get caught up in our heads. Our thoughts spin round and round like an endless record. Suddenly, a quick swipe to your leg jars the needle on your thought turntable. You look down to see your favorite feline staring back at you with a knowing look.

"Send your turntable back to the sixties," she meows!

The interruption brings you back to reality. You grab your car keys, and you and your dog jump into the car and drive away. In the rearview mirror, you see your buddy's snout sticking out the window, the wind blowing his ears back. His goofy expression makes you smile. *What was bothering me again?* you wonder as your stress melts away. You thank your dog because you think it was his idea to get you out of your head. The cat poops on your socks to let you know that it wasn't.

4. Shake it Off

The sky is filled with lightning and it's pouring buckets. You turn to your dog and say, "Sorry buddy, but we can't go out for a walk today."

What does your dog do? He shakes it off.

You didn't see your cat's tail under your shoe, and you accidentally stepped on it. She wails like a banshee and darts under the bed. Twenty minutes later, she's on your lap nudging her head against your hand for a scratch between her ears.

Cats and dogs are the best role models I know for showing forgiveness. Who will you forgive today?

5. Love is Something You Give

Cats and dogs don't ask us for much, but when it comes to love, they ask us for everything. And why shouldn't they? Our cats and dogs aren't stingy with their own love. They don't keep score on who is giving more or less. When we are in a partnership with them, their affection is unlimited. So take a page from your animals and balance your scale toward the giving of love more than the receiving of it. Who can you appreciate a little more today? A coworker, your husband, or your child? Perhaps the person most in need of love is you. This was the case for JoJo, who discovered that even though love may end when someone leaves, when you have a dog, there is a greater love to be had.

KC & JoJo

Several years ago, I was in a relationship. When it fell apart, it left me feeling devastated.

One night, I was kneeling on the kitchen floor as tears flooded down my face. My thoughts were spinning out of control as my mind kept going over and over the details of how things had ended. I felt hopeless and alone. At that moment, KC, my black-and-silver Keeshond, walked up to me and started licking away my tears.

The initials K and C stand for kindness and compassion. I gave him that name to remind myself to be kinder and more compassionate to others. But that night, KC reminded me that I not only needed to be this way with other people but also with myself. If there was one thing that KC was NOT good at it, it was judging others. And judging is just what I was doing to myself. As KC comforted me, I felt he was telling me to stop beating myself over the head for what happened. It was as if he was saying to me, "You're going to be okay, JoJo, we'll get through this." And he was right!

From that moment onward I no longer regarded KC as just a dog. He became my companion and a fellow being truly worthy of his name. In the years that followed, he taught me to be kinder, more compassionate, and less judgmental toward myself. And once I started following his lead, I found that I was better able to extend that kindness and compassion to other beings—humans and animals.

Today, KC's influence has led me to take better care of myself by eating healthier and doing yoga. I even meditate because KC has shown me the importance of living in the present moment.

It's funny—I don't even remember the name of the person I broke up with all those years ago. But I will never forget KC and what he did for me that night.

Animals can feel our deepest emotions and can often help us soothe even our greatest suffering. But what about when we are emotionally cut off from other human beings? The dogs at Jessica's Haven know how to bridge this gap, as you will soon read.

Jessica, Laura & the Jessica's Haven Dogs

The Bed & Biscuit started out as a dog boarding, grooming, and day care facility, but what it has become is so much more.

My business partner's daughter, Jessica, is autistic. She is uncomfortable being around people, and it is difficult for her to engage in conversations. For example, you might ask her, "Jessica, how's your day going?" and she will walk right past you without saying a word. If you ask her again, she might stop and answer quickly, but it's obvious she doesn't want to talk.

In her special needs school, Jessica always thrived, but we knew she wouldn't be happy just bagging groceries once high school ended. We needed to help her find something rewarding that would give her life purpose and meaning.

Jessica has always loved dogs and they have always loved her. Besides the dogs that our clients bring in for us to groom, I also rescue small dogs and try to find them loving homes. Many of these animals come from shelters and other difficult circumstances. Their traumas and life experiences have left many of them shy and scared.

Jessica began to volunteer her time with these rescue dogs. By playing and interacting with them, she helped them gain the socialization skills they needed to be more comfortable around people, which meant they could be more easily adopted.

The rescue proved to be mutual.

I don't know what it is about dogs, but when you stroke them or look into their eyes, they can create a transformation within you. Jessica's change was magical to witness.

When the dogs surrounded Jessica, she was calmer and happier. Instead of breezing past you without a word, she began to engage in conversation, telling you that the dog she was holding was named Oscar, informing you about what games he liked to play, and sharing interesting things about his personality. Sometimes when she was alone with a dog, I would hear her say cute and funny things in full sentences: "Oh, look at how you are wagging your tail. You are so cute."

In time, it became clear that Jessica was not only good at connecting with dogs, she could make them look good, too! Jessica could bathe and blow-dry them, as well as clean their ears—the prep work that needed to be done before I could groom them. In short order, Jessica became a groomer's assistant, and her confidence blossomed.

Today, Bed & Biscuit has joined forces with Jessica's Haven & Rescue. Here, other special needs young adults can follow in Jessica's footsteps and learn the art of dog grooming, while at the same time giving unwanted dogs an opportunity to socialize with humans and find their forever homes.

Recently, a group of kids from a local college's special day program began coming over after school. The first week, they just stood in the lobby. The following week, they got as far as sitting with the dogs. Eventually, the boys warmed up to the animals—except for one boy, who still refused to engage with them. He sat on his chair while the other boys sat on the ground. But one day, a fluffy little white Chihuahua named Esme jumped on his lap, put her paws on his chest, and started kissing his chin. The boy's hands went up in surprise, but then he began to giggle.

"Is that scary?" I asked him.

The big grin on his face told me it wasn't. "It's like being on a roller coaster!" he said with excitement.

It's the little things like this that happen all of the time that tell me what we are doing is a good thing . . . a very good thing.

Paws for your Prescription!

From the office of
Nurse Kitty Wiskas and Dr. Harry Friend

1. To build a high IQ, study more. To have a higher EQ—
yawn more! Empathy is key when it comes to Emotional
Intelligence, and we have a lot of it to give.

2. Do you know a child who is autistic? An autism
assistance dog may be what that little human needs to
learn how to connect with others.

3. Do you want to know what your EQ is? Go online and
search the web for "EQ tests." Carlyn tells us you will
find some there that you can take for free.

COMING UP: You've learned how your cats and dogs can be superheroes when it comes to improving your emotional well-being. Are
you ready to become a hero in your own story now? The secret to
finding your inner hero lies on the pages to come!

CHAPTER 14

The Hero Inside and The Hero Beside

"I think dogs are the most amazing creatures; they give unconditional love. For me, they are the role model for being alive."

—Gilda Radner

Hero with a Thousand Faces, scholar Joseph Campbell's signature book, delves into the powerful influence of myth on the way we live. The timeless stories we all know may have different storytellers and they may reach us through various mediums, but all of them tell the story of *the Hero*.[88]

Every Hero, Campbell writes, must pass through several stages of hardship, strife, and danger. They come face to face with their darkest shadows, sometimes in the form of dragons, demons, and villains. Sometimes these forces prove challenging to recognize, like a shape-shifter, an old friend, or even the hero themselves. The journey can become so challenging that the Hero can reach a point of desperation and lose sight of hope. But the Hero is not alone. Friends, wise teachers, and sometimes even the gods themselves provide him with assistance along the way. And once the Hero has successfully passed through each stage of their journey, the way he views the world changes forever.

Joseph Campbell's insights transformed a generation of artists, writers, and filmmakers, most notably George Lucas, who used the stages of the Hero's journey to create the *Star Wars* film series. The Hero's journey is not just a story to be read on a Kindle or viewed on a movie screen; it has a much deeper significance than that. The truth is, we are each the Hero of our own journey. We are the protagonist in our own life's story.

Each of us is at a different stage in the journey. Some of us are at the beginning, unaware that events can challenge us and change our world at any time. Others are farther along, facing repeated tests that make us wonder if we are ever going to get through to the other side. And then there are those of us who are full-on battling our inner dragons—and feeling like we're losing.

When you are feeling particularly vulnerable or wondering if this is all there is in life . . . take a step back, breathe (a lot), and refocus. Remind yourself that even heroes are human, they struggle, and they suffer. At times, heroes even feel like giving up. But in the end, they don't.

THE HERO BESIDE

If you can't yet see yourself as a hero, then look into your cat's or dog's eyes. How do they see you? The adoration staring back at you should not be taken lightly, denied, or ignored. Every animal I've ever had the fortune of living with has reminded me that I am a hero in his or her eyes. I may not be perfect, but what hero is? Even our onscreen superheroes always have a weakness that in the end often results in the birth of an even greater strength. Our imperfections and flaws are what make us interesting and unique. Have the courage to look into the eyes of your animal friends and you may witness your own brilliance.

When I spoke to Dr. Ulka Agarwal, MD, a staff psychiatrist at The George Washington University Colonial Health Center, about animals' abilities to help us discover the hero inside, she shared this story about Tina and her emotional support dog, Toby.

Toby & Tina

Tina was a thirty-year-old patient who lived alone in a tiny apartment and suffered from panic attacks and suicidal thoughts. Throughout her entire life, Tina had been severely criticized by her family. Their judgment had created an inner voice in her mind that constantly told Tina, "You're not good enough."

Tina's confidence was undermined by that voice and over the years she grew depressed and anxious. Her fears kept her from interacting with other people. She had no friends, no partner; she had never even been on a date before. When Tina rode the subway, loud voices would make her so frightened that she would begin to cry. Her crying would sometimes become so uncontrollable that the police would come and take her to the emergency room, where doctors would attend to her panic.

Although she was taking medications and going to therapy, Tina's isolation from other people continued to escalate. She knew she needed help . . . and soon.

As a young girl, whenever Tina felt the sharpness of her mother's criticism, she would seek solace with the one friend she knew wouldn't judge her: the family dog. Playing and being with her dog helped Tina find peace during those difficult early days. Now she wondered if having a dog could help her find some happiness.

When Tina rescued Toby from animal control, just before he was about to be euthanized, her life changed. Toby, a two-year-old husky, needed lots of exercise, attention, and playtime every single day. His needs forced Tina out of her comfort zone and into the world, which until then she had been closing herself away from. Their long hikes together decreased her anxiety and significantly improved her mood. Now, instead of feeling traumatized in the subway, Tina would reach out to Toby. Just touching him would get her to breathe easier and calm herself. These moments allowed Tina to collect her thoughts and realize there was nothing to fear. With Toby as her emotional support dog, Tina could get herself to school and move forward with the rest of her day. Tina and Toby saved each other.

Tina no longer thinks of suicide. Her confidence has grown so much that she has even taken on some leadership roles at her college. Her family of four-legged support has also grown; she now has two cats and two hamsters in addition to Toby. Tina still may have a bad day after talking to her human family, and as she tells me about it, she might start crying. But now, when I ask her about her animals, she gets a big smile on her face and tells me about all of the things she's going to do for them. Feeding them, cleaning their cages, *and taking them for a walk adds purpose to Tina's life. She knows that her animals are there for her, and she is there for them.*

I received a card in the mail not so long ago. Inside was a photo of Tina and Toby on top of a mountain they had just hiked together. Because of Toby, Tina has scaled mountains. She has come a long, long way.

The important point here is this: If you're feeling like life is hitting you hard from all sides, try to remember that battling dragons is the way that we uncover the hero inside of us. It is also crucial to remember that if you're an animal lover, you are not alone on this journey.

At the end of a 1988 interview with journalist Bill Moyers on PBS, Joseph Campbell uttered three words that resonated so profoundly with those that heard it that they have been a catchphrase ever since: "Follow your bliss."

By encouraging us to follow our bliss, Joseph Campbell reminds us to figure out what our passion is, what feeds our soul and makes us happy, and to not be afraid to follow it. And who better than our animal friends to pick up the scent of joy and invite their favorite humans along for the ride? Campbell may have spent his entire life studying religions and myths to discover a truth that cats and dogs have inherently known since the beginning of time.

If you find yourself going through a hard time, battling dragons at every turn, look to your animal friends and seek their wisdom like 8 did with his dog, Poppy. You may find that they are the ideal heroes to walk beside you, even when the journey is three thousand miles long.

Poppy & 8

My name is 8. I'm called that because when I was born, my dad added up the numbers in my birthdate and the number came out to an 8. He said that in eastern cultures, 8 is a lucky number, and that was much more interesting than calling me Rick.

My wife got breast cancer when she was twenty-seven. Our dog, Poppy, would lay next to her in bed and growl when the morphine bag got low and beeped. One day, I heard her growl and ran upstairs—but when I got there, I knew something was wrong. I went over to my wife and saw that she was gone. She was too young to die.

When she was alive, my wife took care of five cats that belonged to our neighbors who got too old or sick and had to go to nursing homes. Once a month my wife would pack the car with the cats and take them for a visit to the nursing home so they could be together again. That's the kind of person she was.

My wife's name? I'd rather not say. She was part Cherokee, and told me that the sooner that I could forget her face after she died, the faster she'd be able to go where she needed to go. The last thing I could do for my wife was to respect her wishes. And her wishes were for me not to dwell on her. The only way I could let her go was to forget her name.

My insurance company told me that my wife must have had cancer before we got married so they wouldn't cover her medical bills. I used all my savings to pay for her care and I lost everything. It was a traumatic time for me, and if it wasn't for Poppy I'd be dead.

I was contemplating suicide one night, but when I fell asleep I dreamed about Poppy. She was at our front door, and I thought she was waiting for my wife to come home, but then I realized, it was me she was waiting for. If I were to kill myself, Poppy would be waiting for me for the rest of her life. I couldn't do that to her. She's my best friend.

My wife had always wanted to visit the West Coast, and I guess when you live in Virginia you can only go west. So I decided to trade in my tombstone for a walk across the country. I put the little money I had left into a college fund for my stepdaughter, found good homes for the cats, and began walking from Virginia to Washington, nearly three thousand miles.

When you're walking it's hard to think about the past. You think instead about how heavy your pack is, and how much your feet are hurting. I was carrying four pounds of dog food and ten pounds of water. We had a hard time walking through Colorado in the winter. Poppy is small, a Peach Tree Coon, and couldn't walk through the snow, so I would tie her to my pack and walk with her that way until I could set her down again.

Along the way, I found jobs doing things like helping guys in Kansas throw bales of hay on a truck. When you're walking and living like that, you're not *worrying about how you'll feel tomorrow, or how you felt yesterday. You're feeling what you're feeling now, and you're either enjoying it or not.*

It took us fourteen months to get to California, but when we finally made it, we settled in Fairfax. I picked up litter and made a sign for my bucket that said "Donation-powered litter control." The people in the community respected my work, so now I have a good job cleaning a local bar.

I don't call myself homeless; I like to say that I live outside. Honestly, I prefer to live this way. I sleep under a tarp that I can open so I can read in the sunlight, or I can close it off at night so it's like an igloo. The most expensive thing I own is a portable DVD player, because I like watching movies that I get from the local library. My favorite movie is The Shawshank Redemption; it's about being trapped, and then realizing you're not as trapped as you thought you were.

I learned from Poppy that you don't have to be picky to be happy. It doesn't matter to her whether we sleep outside or inside. She's not picky about her food, either; she's just as happy eating a rotten fish as she is a fresh can of salmon. Sleeping on a bed or sleeping on the ground . . . if you're sleepy enough, you can sleep anywhere. That's how Poppy is. I was pretty picky once, but not now. I don't want a house anymore; all I want is my dog.

I have PTSD, and Poppy can tell when I'm not happy. When I'm feeling bad, she lies on my lap and watches me and likes to be petted. Sometimes that makes me feel better right away; some days it takes longer. Poppy helps me not to fret over the small things. We worry because it's what we're taught. Luckily, no one ever taught Poppy that.

Poppy has no regrets, but she doesn't do anything that she needs to regret, either. We should be more like animals instead of making them act like us. I mean, you can bang your head against a wall about technology, or you can be like a dog. The most advanced technology Poppy has is the stick she fetches.

I don't go to sleep at night expecting to wake up the next day. It's a happy coincidence each day that I do. But I love to wake up and see Poppy lying next to me and watching me. I can't tell you whether dogs love or not, but I know I love her. We're best friends. She's more like an EMT than a doctor; more like a paramedic than a surgeon. Poppy has kept me alive.

Paws for your Prescription!

From the office of
Nurse Kitty Wiskas and Dr. Harry Friend

1. What stage of the Hero's journey are you on? Wherever you are, there we will be too.

2. When you are feeling like a zero, look into our eyes and you will see what we see: a Hero.

3. Are you alone on your journey? If we're in a shelter, we're alone too. Shall we journey through life together?

4. For a glimpse of all of the two- and four-legged heroes that you have met throughout these pages, go to our online photo gallery:www.AnimalHumanHealth.com/gallery/.

COMING UP: With the help of your animal friends, you've come to realize that your emotional body is just as important to nourish as its physical counterpart. You've learned that thoughts can create and destroy and that your words have the power to diminish or enhance your well-being. You've even discovered that the body has a hidden language of its own. Are you ready to access something even greater? Your Extraordinary Spirit awaits!

PART III

Your Extraordinary Spirit

If a dog were my doctor or a cat my nurse,
what advice would they give me?

"If a dog were my doctor, he would advise: whenever you find something you like, roll in it; chase your tail at least three miles a day; only yell at something smaller than you; sniff before you eat; nap whenever and wherever you can; and most important, use love as your default emotional response."

—Gary Rydstrom, director and seven-time Academy Award
winning sound designer

CHAPTER 15

Stepping Through the Comfort Zone

"A dog doesn't care if you're rich or poor, smart or dumb.
Give him your heart . . . and he'll give you his."

—Milo Gathema

When Neo took the blue pill from Morpheus in the film *The Matrix*, his world changed. Neo could have chosen the red pill, and in doing so remained in the comfort of the life he knew. But instead he chose to pursue the truth, and in swallowing the blue pill, he was thrust out of his comfort zone, became a hero, and saved the world.

The Matrix is a movie and Neo is a fictional character, but the story is also a thought-provoking allegory. Every day we choose our life: we go to work, buy a house, and build our families. You may be content with this life, but do you ever find yourself wondering: *Could I do more? Be more? What if?* We dream of writing a novel, traveling to a foreign land, talking to the guy with the dark brown eyes from the coffee shop . . . but the years pass and the book goes unwritten, your passport remains devoid of stamps, and Brown Eyes just got back from his honeymoon—with your roommate.

You don't have to give up everything that makes you comfortable to be extraordinary. But if there is a voice in the back of your head daring you to take a step in the direction of your dreams, maybe it's time to listen.

THE COMFORT ZONE DEFINED

The comfort zone is an emotional state where we function with ease and without stress. It is where we feel the most comfortable and at home. The term itself may have originated in reference to the temperature zone in which we feel the most comfortable: sixty-seven to seventy-eight degrees.[89]

The amygdala, an almond-shaped mass inside our brain, controls our comfort zone. During our ancestral times, the amygdala would alert us to an unseen predator by making us feel enough fear or anxiety to climb a tree or hide out in a cave until the threat had passed. Like a sixth sense, the amygdala could steer us clear of danger and keep us and our loved ones safe.

Today, most of us have traded the dangers of the wild for concrete jungles. But our amygdalas continue to generate uncomfortable feelings to keep us within our comfort zones—and this survival mechanism exacts a price from our personal growth.

I once saw a short film where the lead character attempted to step out of his comfort zone by trying something new until an evil villain, who lived in his brain, began firing anxiety, fear, and doubt at his amygdala. Within seconds, the character had lost his motivation to change his life and was sitting back on the couch, eating a cheeseburger, and putting off losing those fifty pounds for yet another year.

Judgments, criticisms, and negative thoughts—our own and those of other people—chain us to our comfort zones. As a consequence, we begin to second-guess ourselves and rationalize why we can't take a risk: *It's not a good time, I don't have the money, I'm too old, I'm too fat, I'm not good enough.* Our comfort zones may feel cozy, but being tethered to them can keep us from finding and living the life of our dreams.

5 BENEFITS TO BUSTING OUT OF YOUR COMFORT ZONE

- Helps you break out of a boring and repetitive routine
- Challenges your brain and enables you to learn new things
- Offers you an opportunity for more adventure
- Increases your ability to deal with the unexpected

- Moves you from a place of feeling limited to a more expanded way of living

Skydiving out of a plane, bungee jumping, and swimming with sharks may not be for you, and that is 100 percent okay! Small steps away from your comfort zone are just fine. Think about it: If you take one small step every day, that's 365 steps in a year. Who might you become in one year? How will your transformation benefit your loved ones, your community, and the world? And who might be a great guide, supportive buddy, and loyal companion as you take your 365 steps towards embodying an extraordinary spirit? You guessed it!

The beauty of our cats and dogs is that they help us to become better just through their presence and companionship—quietly, lovingly, and without fanfare. The following tips reflect a few simple yet profound ways that our cats and dogs can inspire us to step out of our comfort zones and toward an extraordinary life.

TACKLING YOUR COMFORT ZONE WITH THE 5 C'S

1. Curious Kitty

Have you ever watched your cat stare at an empty paper sack in the middle of the floor? Suddenly their whiskers flick, their tail darts back and forth, and then . . . POUNCE! The sack is crushed. Then, as if they could care less, they step off the bag and walk away. This game is a fun reminder that although a curious mind may lead to an empty sack, it can also lead to something unexpected. Saying hello to a stranger who could become your new BFF, taking up archery, or eating Ethiopian food (in Ethiopia!) are some of many possibilities that we can create when we allow ourselves to be curious and POUNCE right out of our comfort zone!

2. Cherish the Game and Relish the Prize

Have you ever noticed how much dogs enjoys playing fetch? They revel in the anticipation, they love the game itself, and when they finally leap into the air and catch the ball, they enjoy that just as much.

So when you step out of your comfort zone and lose those twenty pounds, or dance out of your comfort zone and into a tango class, or jump out of your comfort zone and down the zip line, don't forget to enjoy the process *and* celebrate your accomplishments.

3. Challenge Yourself

I leaped way out of my comfort zone when I adopted my dog Roxy. She lunged, she bit, she was out of control. Still, I was committed to helping her find a normal way of life. Fortunately, I found teachers who taught me that to be a true pack leader with my dogs, one must be a *benevolent* leader.

Because Roxy had a history of neglect and mistreatment, I had to challenge myself to understand her better. The challenge has made me more confident and capable, and a better animal guardian. My dog challenged me to step out of my comfort zone, and as a result I became a better person. How do your cats and dogs challenge you?

4. Cultivate Daily Adventures

Adventure is the golden ticket out of your comfort zone. But you don't have to go on an African photo safari or climb Mt. Everest. Instead, take your dog for a hike on a new trail, and while you're there, have an adventure of the senses: smell the aroma of the damp earth after it rains, listen to the musical sound of a distant creek, taste the flavor of the air on your tongue, feel the ridges of the tree bark under your fingertips, and watch how your dog's fur glistens in the sun. These moments can bring you into your *Now*, and it's an adventure you can go on every single day.

5. Courage in Small Steps

Every step out of the comfort zone takes courage. The first time I spoke publicly, I was so nervous that my voice disappeared. My lips kept moving, but a frog had apparently found refuge in my throat, and his croak was now addressing the thirty acupuncture students sitting in front of me.

Afterward, as the fever of humiliation burned red on my cheeks, I crawled into bed with Cody, my orange tabby. Cody licked away my tears and rubbed against me, insisting I stroke his silky fur. His purr soothed my shame and told me, "It's not that bad, kid. I still love you. Try again." And I did.

Eventually I became a member of Toastmasters, an organization that teaches public speaking. The paralyzing fear I used to feel during presentations is now a distant memory, and today I speak regularly to audiences about how our animal friends enhance our well-being. There is no failure when you step out of the comfort zone. The failure is in not trying.

Stepping out of the comfort zone isn't solely reserved for humans. When Max stepped out of his comfort zone and learned to trust Kayle, he healed the trauma of his past and opened the way to a new and amazing life.

Max & Kayle (as told by Margaret Holiday, DC)

Max was a young German shepherd who was kept chained in a backyard in Stockton, California. The people who had Max said they were trying to find him a home. But when Kayle came forward and said she would take him, they told her it would cost her $500, and if she wasn't there in three hours they were going to shoot him. Kayle arrived before the three hours were up and removed Max from his living hell forever.

While in chains, Max sustained a foot injury that eventually made him chew off his own foot. Animals feel emotions strongly, so to chew off your own foot is just as unimaginable for a dog to do as it would be for a human. We hear about this with foxes or other animals who get caught in traps. They are so afraid and in such extreme pain that they will chew off a limb to escape. We don't know exactly what happened that made Max do this to himself, but whatever it was, he probably did it to save his own life.

Luckily, this experience, as terrible as it was, didn't define Max. In Kayle's home, Max was surrounded by a love he had never known, and her devotion, care, and commitment to him allowed him to heal in body, mind, and spirit.

I think there is a great lesson for humans here about letting go of the past and living in the moment. It's about the simplicity of being with what is happening now. We humans get hooked into our stories, but animals live in the moment instead of dwelling in the past.

Max feels the friendship, dedication, and love that Kayle has given him, and he seems unconcerned with his own physical disability or the horrors he once endured. He has simply let go of them and is walking into the future with his new guardian. This future is bright and lovely because of Max's ability to let go and not harbor a grudge, and his willingness to step out of his comfort zone and trust again.

With a house full of cats and dogs, I could not bring another animal into our home without upsetting the balance of the other two- and four-legged creatures in my life. But when I met Mack and saw his situation, I could not turn my back on him. As Mack braved going out of his own comfort zone, this unforgettable dog led me out of mine.

Mack & Carlyn

He reminded me of Cujo: the rabid dog in the horror movie by Stephen King. At the shelter where I volunteered, when the dogs saw a human, they would run up to the front of their cages, desperate for affection and hoping to be walked—but not Mack. He would slink to the back of his enclosure and his massive, eighty-five-pound, black lab–pit bull body would disappear into the darkness. No one wanted to go near him.

Eventually, I'd had enough. I could no longer bear to see Mack in his cage, unwalked, unloved, and passed over for adoption week after week. My concern for him outweighed my fear of him, so I took a deep breath, opened his cage, and stepped inside.

I was nervous at first but decided it was a good day to "fake it until I make it," so I pretended to be just fine. As Mack growled, I spoke softly to him, tossing treats at him with every step. I even sang him a tune, though I will admit it was a bit out of key. I visited Mack for several days, offering food and Bruce Springsteen songs, but my affection was continually met with resistance.

One day I reached the rear enclosure and was surprised to find that Mack tolerated my touch. But when my leash went around his neck, it was more than he could stand. Mack became a bucking bronco, pulling hard, falling behind, and then refusing to budge. Walking Mack was torture—for both of us. Later I found out that Mack and his brother, Riley, who lived in the cage next to him, had spent most of their two years living in a car. They'd never been walked or socialized and were therefore, fearful of people, loud noises, and anything out of the usual. Since walking Mack and Riley was out, and cars were what they knew, my Volvo station wagon became their chariot, and the local dog park their haven.

Mack and Riley loved their outings, and the more they got out, the more their demeanors improved. Despite their progress, however, the shelter owner told me that these dogs would never get adopted and they needed their cages for other dogs who actually stood a chance of finding a home. When she said she was planning on euthanizing them, I officially became Mack and Riley's guardian and spent the next six months trying to find them their forever homes.

Finally, one splendid Sunday, a mom and her young daughter came to the shelter and fell in love with Riley, and despite his fears, they brought him home.

Mack's day finally came too. But his forever home would not be in Los Angeles, where we lived, but in Helena, Montana, a three-day car ride away.

Driving through freezing temperatures alone and with a fearful dog was not an idea I relished, but I knew this was Mack's only chance. So off we went, listening to Bruce Springsteen's greatest hits and watching the terrain change from green to brown to white along the way. By the time the snow flurries came, there were no other cars on the highway. I began to sweat. As the flurries grew thicker, I sweated even more. My mechanic had told me that if the temperature reached zero degrees, my car might stop dead. So when the temperature gauge dropped to one degree, I held my breath and found myself saying forgotten prayers I had once said as a child.

Finally, Helena showed her face in the distance and I began to breathe again.

John and Danzel, a sweet older couple, invited us into their home when we arrived at their door. Mack reciprocated by jumping on top of their dining room table. I still remember the sound of the dinner plates clanking as Mack's massive frame trembled with fear. I got him down as quickly as possible, and as I turned towards our hosts I fully expected them to show us right out the front door. But they didn't. Instead they laughed and opened their back door, letting in an eager clan of six dogs and cats—Mack's new family.

For the next eight years, Mack lived a full life with a two- and four-legged family who loved, accepted, and appreciated him just as he was. Years later, as Danzel struggled with kidney cancer, she told me what a great friend and companion Mack had been, and how grateful she was that I'd brought him into her life. A year after she passed away, I received a call from Danzel's daughter letting me know that Mack had also died.

Mack forced me out of my comfort zone and into his cage. There he met my comfort zone and raised me one by giving me his trust, perhaps the hardest thing he could have ever offered. We shared three memorable days—staying in cheap motels, eating food that wasn't very good for us, and watching late-night movies before falling asleep together. If I had ignored Mack at the shelter, Danzel would not have had his love to comfort her during her illness; I would never have had this story to tell; and I wouldn't have the memory of a remarkable dog who reminded me of Cujo—and proved to everyone that all he needed was a second chance at life.

Paws for your Prescription!

From the office of
Nurse Kitty Wiskas and Dr. Harry Friend

1. Feeling bored or going through a rut? Try something new with your animal buddies. Go camping, take up jogging, or learn a new game together.

2. Take a step out of your comfort zone and meet someone new. Dog parks are great places to meet other like-minded humans, as are cat cafés.

3. Challenge your comfort zone by learning a new language—and that includes our languages! Get past "sit," "stay," and "fetch," and learn to have more meaningful communications with us. Look for positive reinforcement trainers, insightful books, and fun videos to teach you what we may be trying to tell you.

COMING UP: Now you understand how getting out of your comfort zone, and feeling the support of your animal friend at your side, can springboard you into a more extraordinary life. But did you know that your cats and dogs can also inspire your inner Picasso?

CHAPTER 16

Your Creative Animal

"God is really another artist. He invented the giraffe, the elephant, and the cat. He has no real style. He just goes on trying other things."

—Pablo Picasso

We are all born to be creative, whether or not we believe we have talent. We arrive in this world with imagination and unique qualities that make us who we are. A poet infuses us with the magic of a moment caught in words, an architect gives birth to a structure that fills us with awe, and a musician leaves their song imprinted on our hearts. Creativity has many expressions, though; you don't have to be a great artist to connect with your creative spark. Whether it's choosing the style of clothes you wear, the variety in the meals you prepare, or how you raise your children, every day you have the opportunity to be creative in your life. Your creativity is the footprint you'll leave upon the world when your third act ends.

Pablo Picasso, perhaps the most influential artist of the twentieth century, believed that all children were born to be artists. The problem, he felt, was how to remain an artist once you grew up. Today, just as in Picasso's time, most of us are told from day one who we are and what road to follow. We hear and heed everyone's voice but our own. Some of us strive to create, but if the inspiration doesn't emanate from our authentic voice, what we produce may seem lifeless, or like it belongs to someone else (which it often does).

How, then, do we find and express our unique voice? How do we access our creative spark and allow it to catch fire?

FOUR-LEGGED MUSES

The ancient Greeks believed that nine goddesses, or *Muses*, were the source of human inspiration. They also believed that their creativity came from divine spirits called daemons. Socrates, the famous Greek philosopher, said that he had been guided by a daemon since childhood, and this voice guided him in all things. The Muses and daemons were concepts that inspired and explained the creative spark in Greek culture. But do our Muses have to be goddesses?

Leonardo da Vinci, considered to be one of the greatest artists of all time, was a Renaissance man—skilled not just in painting but also in architecture, botany, and science. He also conceived of the idea for the first parachute and sketched the first helicopter.

Da Vinci lived during the fifteenth century, long before our current love affair with cats and dogs. Even so, he studied and drew the anatomy of animals, and was even quoted as once saying, "The smallest feline is a masterpiece." He was also a vegetarian because of his concern for all animals.[90] A cat or a dog may not have inspired the Mona Lisa, but it appears that Da Vinci's life was influenced by them.

In the book *Pawprints of History*, author Stanley Coren describes how Florence Nightingale once came to the aid of a sheepdog named Cap. Cap was about to be hung by a shepherd who could not afford to treat the dog's injured leg. When Nightingale heard the news of Cap's fate, she grew so upset that she took on the responsibility of his care and nursed him back to health. Florence Nightingale is considered the founder of modern nursing, and Cap the dog was her first patient.[91] Nightingale was not an artist in the conventional sense, but her friendship and concern for Cap the dog led her to become the legendary nurse that we associate with self-sacrifice and compassion. Florence Nightingale's art was caring for other people, and it became her legacy.

Artists Andy Warhol, Norman Rockwell, and composer Frederic Chopin all shared a close relationship with and were inspired in their work by cats and dogs.[92],[93] Today, we see heavy metal rockers cuddling with their kitties, award-winning actors like Tom Hardy walking the red carpet with their dogs, and cats perched on the shoulders of presidents. And who can forget films like *Lassie*, *Marley and Me*, and *Hachi: A Dog's Tale*, where a dog's devotion and love breaks open our hearts? Or cats, like Puss in Boots from the movie *Shrek*, who make us laugh to the point of tears?

A Dog's Purpose spent over a year on the *New York Times* bestseller list. It is a novel told from a dog's perspective—a dog who keeps being reborn until he can figure out his purpose. The book touched me so deeply that I asked author W. Bruce Cameron to share what inspired him to write his book, and he told me about Cammie.

Cammie & Bruce

My very first dog was named Cammie. She always exposed me to the brighter side of things, inspired me with her joy, and gave me great stability during my childhood. Many years after she passed, I was riding my bike in Colorado when I saw a dog on the side of the road. I always stop and talk to dogs, and as I interacted with this Australian shepherd, I realized how much she reminded me of Cammie. Something in her eyes, the way she looked at me, the way she wagged her tail and put her paw up, was just like Cammie used to do.

I had this odd sense that I was interacting with my first dog, and I began to wonder: What if dogs never really die? What if what we think is instinct is actually memory? And if dogs were reborn, what would that look like from a dog's perspective? Years later, that encounter propelled me into writing A Dog's Purpose.

We often ignore what we know to be true—that true love never dies, and that our real friends are always with us in some way. People tend to get caught up in their day-to-day stuff and don't really pay attention to those important lessons. Dogs pull us out of our dour fixation on things we can do nothing about; politics, for example. But for a dog you pick up a stick or a ball, and you wave it around in front of her nose, and that brings real joy into your dog's life and into yours. These are the moments that make you human. That kind of love, affection, and fun is the whole point of life. Dogs remind us of that every single day.

Writing isn't the only art that can be inspired by our animal friends. If you're more into the visual arts, you might be interested in reading about how Sunny and Orchid inspire their guardian, Barbara, to take her paintings to a higher level, and in the process touch the lives of countless children.

Sunny, Orchid & Barbara

I've been a professional watercolor artist for the last thirty years, and an animal lover all of my life. I combine my two loves by teaching an animal kindness art class to young children in Maui, where I live. During class, the kids are taught about the animals they choose to paint, like giraffes, gorillas, and fish. They also get guidance in the care and responsibility for their own animal companions. Learning about the animals and their environment helps the children be better guardians of their planet.

It all began when I was painting the view from my lanai late one afternoon. The sun was setting over the ocean, and in the distance was the island of Kahoolawe. All around, the royal poinciana trees were blooming with orange flowers. Suddenly, both my cats jumped onto the banister and sat exactly in front of where I was painting, even though we were twenty feet above the ground. Sunny, an orange tabby, sat looking out over the ocean, but Orchid, who was a tiger calico, looked directly at me. Every time I looked up from the canvas I'd meet her eyes.

When a cat looks in your eyes, they are giving you a gift. That day, Orchid's gift was to influence what I was painting, as well as give me the idea to teach children about art and kindness by painting images of animals. Orchid inspired me without using words or even a meow. The three of us sitting together in the quiet hours was magical. And the painting turned out great; it's one of my best, and I'm so proud of it.

I've been teaching my animal kindness class to children for ten years now. The cats inspire the children's creativity, give them more confidence, and help them to be calmer and happier. At the end of every class, each child holds up their work for the other children to see. They share how they've been kind to the animal they've painted, and how they have given them a good home, food and water, and lots of love. Then we put their paintings on Facebook and the kids get excited when they get a lot of "likes." People who see the drawings will often comment on how they feel inspired to be kinder and more compassionate to animals too. The cats are here to inspire the kids, and the kids inspire others through their art. This connection is pretty incredible when you stop to think about it.

Cats and dogs can inspire not only our art but our life's purpose, too. Like Cap did for Florence Nightingale, cats and dogs inspired Ingrid Newkirk toward her vocation. Today, Ingrid is the president and cofounder of People for the Ethical Treatment of Animals (PETA), the largest animal rights organization in the world. During a phone conversation, Ingrid shared with me what inspired her early on in life to accomplish so much on behalf of animals. It all started with dogs and cats.

Ingrid's Story

I was born caring about animals. Our family dog was named Shawnee, and he was bigger than me by far. We grew up together and looked after each other. By watching him, I first came to realize how animals feel, what they like, and what frightens them.

When I was little, we lived in India. I helped my mother in a leper colony, caring for orphan children and stray animals. It was there that I learned that anyone, whether human or animal, can suffer.

When I was eight, a group of people near my home bound a dog's legs and lowered him into a drainage ditch. They filled the dog's mouth with mud and muzzled him, and then laughed and threw clods of dirt at him as they watched him try to get free. A fierce sun beat down on him as he tried to hobble along the ditch. When I heard the laughter and saw what was happening, I made one of our helpers go down and get the dog. When he brought him up to me, I sat with the dog and undid the string around his muzzle. I put my hand into his mouth and started to scrape out the mud, but it had gone down his throat. The dog went into convulsions, and he died sitting in the courtyard of our house, in my arms. This was a turning point for me.

When I was twenty, I came to the US. Not long afterward, my neighbor moved away and left several kittens behind. I took them to the local animal shelter, but the place was horrifying, dirty, and gruff. The animals were so afraid. Then and there, I told myself that I would one day start an animal protection group, but for now I needed to do something about this place in particular. So I quit my job at the brokerage where I worked and went to work in that shelter.

I think we are all here to help each other. Every deed, every action, really does change things. We may never see the result of what we do, but we are changing things when we take any action on behalf of animals.

Inspired by an abused dog and a litter of abandoned kittens, Ingrid Newkirk grew up to be a champion for all animals. Ingrid's art has been her work, and millions of dogs, cats, and other animals have benefited from her passion.

Whether you are an accountant, a fashion designer, or a stay-at-home dad, you are a creator. We may not all be Picasso, O'Keeffe, or Warhol, but each of us has something unique to share, and giving it expression adds value to our life and our world.

If you are an animal lover and have the privilege of living with a cat or a dog, pay attention to the various ways in which they can support, encourage, and infuse your creative spirit. Cats and dogs love us without limit, and their inspiration is also unlimited. You are their masterpiece.

Paws for your Prescription!

From the office of
Nurse Kitty Wiskas and Dr. Harry Friend

1. Did you know that taking a break from being creative can make you even more creative? Finding time to laugh and play with us can help you let go of creativity's number-one enemy: stress.

2. Having a creative block? Whether you are a painter, writer, or plumber, we can help you unlock your genius. Paint us, write about us, or just be quiet with us for a little while, and see what divine inspiration comes your way.

3. Creativity can be a lonely pursuit. When you are in the thick of creating you may not want to engage with other humans. Engage with us instead. Take a break, stroke our fur, feel our joy, and savor the connection.

COMING UP: Love is in the air!

CHAPTER 17

Reinventing Relationships

*"A true cat lover cradles a cat and knows
that nine lives will never be nearly enough."*

—*Unknown*

The quality of our relationships is strongly associated with our well-being. We earthlings are social animals, and we're happiest when we have strong bonds with the people around us. But how do you connect with others when you are shy, self-conscious, or an introvert?

If a cat's got your tongue, a canine pal can be just the remedy to help get you unleashed, and engaged with others of your own species. In fact, dog walking is actually one of the easiest ways to meet new people.[94] And since you need to get a minimum of thirty minutes of exercise everyday anyway, do double duty! Use your dog-walking excursions as an opportunity to smile and say hello to others. If you can't bring yourself to make the first overture, don't worry; studies show that others will probably say hello to you first when they see you strolling with your dog friend.[95]

I walk with my dogs every morning. Half of the time, the people I pass on the way say hello to me; the rest of the time, they ignore me altogether. Instead they say hello to Rudy, Roxy, Dakota, or Teddy—whichever companion I have the fortune to be with at that time. When they finally notice me, they ask my dogs' names, breeds, and ages. Eventually, they may ask my name too.

This experience isn't mine alone. Studies show that animal guardians who move into new neighborhoods make more friends than those without four-legged partners.[96] I didn't know a soul when I first moved into my tightly-knit neighborhood, but enjoying the outdoors with my dogs has introduced me to my community. Hellos have turned into conversations and conversations into friendships. I've even met a neighbor who walks with her cat, and a couple that takes a sunset hike every evening with their rescue donkey . . . and their dachshund. Can you imagine the conversations that get started with these animals by your side?

The need to love and give love is on most people's top ten list. For many it's their deepest desire. Our cats and dogs shower us with the unconditional love and the acceptance we naturally crave. And in caring for their needs, they show us how rewarding it can feel to give love in return.

Sheryl Matthys, the founder and CEO of Leashes and Lovers (a network for dog lovers to connect online) and the author of a book by the same name, is an expert on how dogs affect our romantic relationships. I asked her what dogs can teach us about the many aspects of love, and here's what she had to share.

ON FINDING LOVE: "Dogs are the perfect ice-breaker on the way to finding love. They make you feel and look more lovable, because when you walk your dog you are often smiling and feel happier. Looking positive can make it easier to meet somebody new. Dogs are great love magnets; they help attract dog lovers to other dog lovers."

ON KEEPING LOVE: "Dogs are your number one fans. They are completely loyal and you can count on them to be there for you. Dogs don't want to trade you in for a younger version of yourself, and they don't need you to lose five pounds or drive a fancy car. They look at you with so much admiration. It's hard to go wrong in their eyes. What if we always looked that way at the person we are dating or married to? What if we always saw the best in one another? Life is tough and we can all use a cheerleader to help us along the way. I think a lot of people would have deeper relationships and would feel more respected if they took the time to accept themselves the way their dogs accept them."

ON LEAVING LOVE BEHIND: "Dogs are forgiving and can wipe the slate clean with ease. My experience with rescued greyhounds has shown me that even if they have lived a completely different or difficult life before they have gotten to me, they don't hold on to that baggage. They come fresh and ready to love you. They don't just sit there and feel sorry for themselves. Dogs are forgiving and ready to trust when love comes again."

ON YOUR OWN RELATIONSHIP: "Dogs have taught me the importance of being there for one another and listening to what each of us has to say. Even when you have nothing to say to one another, your quiet presence can have a huge impact on someone. It's about connection and being willing to be present. Our dogs don't sit there and have conversations with us, yet we still feel connected to them."

ON YOUR RELATIONSHIP WITH YOURSELF: "I rescue greyhounds and they are amazing dogs. They are so calm about everything, so gentle and so sweet. These are the things I aspire to be because I'm not usually calm; I'm not always gentle; and I'm not always very sweet. Maybe you hope your dog's qualities rub off on you, or that if people see that about your dog they may think that about you too. I would like to look in the mirror and see that about myself one day, but until then I can at least look at my dog."

Sheryl Matthys demonstrates how dogs can be the loves of our lives while at the same time enhancing our relationships with other humans. On the other side of the coin, I asked Jester and Cody, my feline friends, to share with me—and you—what cats can teach their challenged human friends about relationships. Here are their four top tips for a better love life:

1. RELATIONSHIPS REQUIRE MAINTENANCE. We don't just hang around waiting for love to happen. We make it happen. Every day we seek out the objects of our affection (i.e., you), and soothe you with our warmth, amuse you with our charm, and hypnotize you with our purrs. If there is someone that you love in addition to us, we suggest that you do the same. Love is like catnip: you can never get enough.

2. EVERYONE SHOWS LOVE IN THEIR OWN SPECIAL WAY. Sometimes we purr, sometimes we pounce, sometimes we jump on your shoulders or wrap ourselves around your heads. Sometimes we just watch you from afar with our mesmerizing gaze. Just like humans, all cats are different, so we show our love in different ways. The point is to be there for those you love and to express your love in your unique style.

3. BE SPONTANEOUS AND LEARN TO PLAY. We are standing on a dresser behind a partially open door. We see the human love of our life approaching, totally unaware of their fate. They walk across the threshold, and *pow, pow, pow!*—we hit 'em with a paw and then take off running. If the human is trained well, they will take off after us, racing around our house, making that funny sound they make with their mouths when they are happy. After the excitement is over, we snuggle together or indulge in a yummy treat. Love is grand when you add spontaneity and a dose of playfulness to it, don't you think?

4. LOOK AND FEEL LIKE THE CAT'S PAJAMAS. Just because you've been with someone for a long time doesn't mean you should adopt the grunge look. We cats, being regal beings, spend a lot of our energy making ourselves look splendid. We groom our heads, lick our bodies, and even loofah our cat mate's coat. Surprise your own mate and dress your best, look your best and feel your best. (Catnaps are highly recommended.)

When Liana adopted her cat and dogs, she enjoyed their company—but she had no idea how the unspoken bond that exists between animals and humans would come to support her through the challenging times that lay ahead.

June Bug, Cece, Lucy, Liana & Jason

Several years ago, I was living in New York City and going through a divorce. I'd wake up feeling alone and missing the life I once had. The sadness never lasted long, however, because June Bug, my ruby-colored King Charles Cav-

alier Spaniel, was there to greet me every morning. You just can't look at a dog you love without smiling and feeling their love in return.

Caring for June Bug and making her happy, didn't leave me a lot of time to spend dwelling on the end of my marriage. Taking her for walks in Central Park snapped me out of whatever mood I was in. And since dog people love to talk to other dog people, I made many friends along the way. It didn't matter what kind of day I was having, or if it was raining, sleeting, or snowing; June Bug would turn the worst weather into the most fun event. She reminded me to appreciate life even in the midst of my troubles.

After my divorce I dated a few men, but they weren't into June Bug the way I was, or rather, June Bug wasn't into them. Then Jason came along. The moment he walked through the door and sat on the couch, June Bug climbed onto his head and began licking his face. He loved it, and her, and hardly paid attention to me the whole night. June Bug doesn't like everyone, but she sure loved Jason.

Two months later, Jason and I were engaged, and we moved to San Francisco. Shortly after arriving, Jason's great aunt passed away, leaving us with Lucy, whom she had adopted from a shelter a few months before. Lucy is a black-and-white tuxedo cat whom we fell in love with immediately. She is soft and sweet, and lives on our bed. She also does hilarious things like standing in front of our faces as we try to watch TV. "There's no chance you are going to watch that if I'm around," she seems to say. Lucy was the first cat my husband and I had together, and she helped us bond as a new couple.

I had been volunteering to walk dogs at a dog shelter, but when I became pregnant with our first child, I was put on bed rest. I figured it would be fun to foster a puppy while I was at home. Within twenty-four hours of fostering Cece, a crazy Chihuahua–Jack Russell terrier mix, we knew we were keeping her. Cece tested our ability to parent, our patience, and my own strength at disciplining her (though I must admit I didn't do a good job on the discipline part).

While I was pregnant, June Bug, Lucy, and Cece seemed more attached to me than ever. They wanted to be on my belly all of the time. To this day I am so grateful they were in our lives, because we never could have anticipated what would come to pass.

When it came time for me to give birth, the doctors decided that I needed a C-section. While we were waiting for an operating room to become available, I was wheeled into a hallway and left there. Up to this point our baby, Miller, had been full term and healthy. But after the operation, when I woke up from the anesthesia, the doctors told me Miller was very sick and they were just keeping her alive long enough for me to say good-bye to her. I was in shock.

The first and last moments we held our daughter were filled with an indescribable mixture of tremendous love and complete devastation. I had never felt anything like this level of grief before. Would I be able to get past it? Would I lose my husband because I was so sad? Would I ever heal emotionally from the loss? I couldn't even fathom wanting or loving another child the way I loved Miller.

After something this heartbreaking happens, you don't want to socialize, or go to dinners or parties. Sometimes you don't even want to get out of bed. You can lose your connection to those you love most. Now I understand how people who lose their children can also lose their marriages.

It was our cat and dogs who helped bring Jason and I close again. "Did she poop?" "Did he pee?" "Is she sleeping?" These simple conversations allowed us to focus on something other than ourselves. They gave us something easy and fun to talk about. Even if we didn't want to talk to each other about the big elephant in the room, we could still talk about the love we had for our animals.

Sometimes the animals helped us express ourselves without even having to say a word to one other. Jason would come home from work, and I could see what mood he was in by the way he handled the animals. If he was quietly hugging or stroking them instead of acting like his typical over-the-moon self, I would know he was feeling a little depressed and might need some space.

It's normal for friends and family to want to hug you when you are going through such a difficult period, but grief can make you want to pull away from any physical contact. It's different when it's an animal giving you this kind affection. Their love is pure and their touch feels comforting. In time, holding our cat and dogs helped Jason and me start holding each other again.

Losing Miller could have taken us down a very sad and dark path, but our animals didn't allow it. It was as if they were saying to us, "You have a choice to make: you can either take us outside for a walk, or you can sink into your own oblivion." Because of them, we chose to walk.

The biggest lessons our cat and dogs have taught us are to never give up and to always love. It kills me when I hear about people who have given away their animals. I just don't understand that. Our animal companions would never do that to us. Never. It is a privilege to have an animal share your life. Every day during our hard times, our animals either brought me out of a sad moment or helped me celebrate a happy one. They forced me to feel alive and kept me engaged with the world. Through the most difficult period of my life, my cat and dogs made me feel human again.

(Miller died on December 7, 2013. Otto came into the world two years later.)

Loyalty, spontaneity, acceptance, forgiveness, seeing the best in others, and consoling us through our darkest days are exceptional qualities that our cat and dog friends model for us. Any one of these attributes can take you far in life and make you the envy of your friends. If you find yourself falling short of any of the aforementioned qualities, don't worry; your cat and dog mentors will love you even when you don't do things perfectly. You will always have a second, a third, and a fourth chance with a cat or a dog. As Sheryl Matthys says, "They say doctors don't make house calls anymore, but when you have a dog or cat, you have a doctor or a nurse 24/7."

Paws for your Prescription!

From the office of
Nurse Kitty Wiskas and Dr. Harry Friend

1. Mad at your spouse, annoyed with your boyfriend, or pissed off at your partner? Our advice: talk it out, then go bury your bones. Look to us for inspiration—we're good at making friends, sniffing out foes, and forgiving those we love.

2. Are you looking for romance? Check out Sheryl Matthys's website, LeashesandLovers.com, where you can fetch-a-date. Are you more of a cat aficionado? Go to Meetup.com and connect with feline friends there.

3. Please remember, as much as we like to accompany you everywhere you go, we dogs don't like hot cars and get dangerously overheated quickly. Please leave us at home when it's hot so we can stay cool, safe, and happy.

COMING UP: You went out of your comfort zone and started a conversation with a gal at the cat café. Now you're asking your cat for fashion advice on what to wear on your date. You decide you're feeling pretty darn good, and you look to your animal friends to steer you on to the next step of this incredible journey. Next up? Get ready to give.

CHAPTER 18

To Serve, With Love

*"Friendship isn't about whom you have known the longest . . .
it's about who came and never left your side."*

—Mikaela Tiu

When I was sixteen, my older brother took me to see a movie that forever left its stamp on my soul. For two hours I sat riveted to my seat, eyes glued on the big screen, lost in an adventure called *Star Wars*. Somewhere between storm troopers and Death Stars I had the thought, *I want to do that!*

Eight years later I found myself doing *just that* as an assistant film editor at Lucasfilm. Working on movies allowed me to meet fascinating people, engage with celebrities, and travel to interesting places. But eventually the stresses of my 24/7 workweek began to replace the original thrill. As I ticked off the years I began to wonder, *Is this what my life will always be like?*

Twenty years later I finally burned out with my film career, and I enrolled in a master's degree program in Chinese medicine. I juggled work, school, and a new family. Six years later, I took a five-hour licensing exam, which, to my surprise, I passed with high marks.

On the day I got the news, I went for a celebratory walk with Roxy. As a reward the universe sent a stray dog across my path. Immediately, I made a beeline for the confused creature, as did a neighbor I had never met before. After we found the dog's home, and returned him to his grateful guardian, my new friend asked if I would volunteer to walk rescue dogs with her at a local shelter. I told her I was pretty busy but agreed to help her for one hour the following day.

As promised, the next morning I met Elaine at the shelter. The next day I showed up again . . . and then the next day after that. Two weeks later, Elaine and I found ourselves at the shelter in the dark after having spent eight hours walking sixty-five dogs. Our feet were aching, our stomachs were growling, and we were caked with sweat. When nine o'clock rolled around we were gently escorted by a shelter worker to the front gate and asked to go home.

It was hard to sleep that night knowing that four dogs hadn't gone for what may have been their only walk of the week. On the following morning, as soon as the doors opened, Elaine and I showed up and walked the last four dogs.

Walking dogs eight hours a day was not something I could do every day, or ever again, for that matter. So I offered to become the shelter's volunteer coordinator. My self-appointed job was to recruit others to help us walk and play with the dogs while they waited for their forever families. Or, if the volunteers were cat lovers, they were invited to visit the cat area and socialize with them. The volunteers were of different ages, races, and genders; there were engineers, housewives, students, and members of the military. The Lynnes, Georges, Tanyas, Vickies, Theresas, and Elaines who came together during that time formed an alliance of common purpose: to create a better and happier life for our animal friends. Our service to those animals bonded us as a group.

During the time I volunteered at the shelter, I lost fifteen pounds, gave up a lifelong addiction to sugar, and opened my wellness practice, Modern Alchemy Acupuncture & Nutritional Counseling. Volunteering also taught me that transformation has many paths, and service is one of them, especially when a cat or dog is in the brew.

SERVICE SERVES THE SERVER

From an early age, humans are hardwired to care for others. But did you know that giving benefits you just as much as the person you are giving to? Focusing on another's needs, especially when those needs are greater than our own, increases our empathy. And as we know from Chapter 14, empathy feeds our Emotional Intelligence stockpile (and we can always use plenty of that). Giving of ourselves, and our time, is a useful reality check reminding us that someone who is down and out could just as easily be *us* under different circumstances.

The following are some of the rewards awaiting you, should you accept the life-enhancing opportunity that service to another provides.

5 BENEFITS OF SERVING

- Heightens our compassion for others
- Can reduce anxiety and depression for both the giver and the receiver
- Benefits well-being for both parties
- Enhances the immune system
- Gives the giver a sense of purpose

A dog can be taught to heel, but when we allow our dogs to be our doctors and our cats to be our nurses, they can teach us to *heal.* Not only do we benefit by helping others, as animal lovers we can also get an extra dose of well-being when those we serve are our furry friends. If you've ever volunteered in a shelter, you know that nothing can transform a bad day faster than being greeted by wagging tails, adoring eyes, and oodles of wet snouts. And when the day comes that your shelter friends who may have suffered at the hands of abuse, neglect, or abandonment get their second chance at love in the arms of a lonely child, an excited couple, or a veteran in need of their own second chance at love, you will find your heart filled with a sweetness that is hard to rival.

There are many types of service, support, and therapy cats and dogs helping their guardians with a variety of needs. Service dogs are trained to perform tasks for people with disabilities such as Parkinson's disease, seizures, and mobility impairments. Diabetic service cats and dogs alert you to a rise in your glucose levels through their keen sense of smell. Hearing service dogs warn their guardian of a siren they might not otherwise be aware of on a busy street. Emotional support cats and dogs provide companionship and non-judgmental, positive regard for people challenged by emotional issues. Therapy cats and dogs give affection and comfort to people in clinics, hospitals, and rest homes. From cats helping veterans with PTSD to allergy-alert dogs, service animals abound.

While I was researching this book, Margaret Holiday, DC, the gifted animal chiropractor who makes an appearance in Chapters 8 and 15, invited me to meet her client Anne Marie. When we arrived at Anne Marie's apartment, Bodhidharma, a blackish-gray tabby named after a famous Buddhist monk, greeted us at the door. After a quick sniff-check and gentle chirrup, the stately kitty allowed us in.

Anne Marie is confined to a wheelchair. Multiple sclerosis has rendered her unable to move any part of her body. Because she can only manage small breaths of air at a time, her voice is strained and her words come with tremendous effort. But her eyes tell the story of the love and devotion she has for her "companion, guide, and best friend" Bodhidarma.

Bodhidarma & Anne Marie

Anne Marie: "I went to the Marin Humane Society to adopt a kitten, but then I saw Bodhidharma, a fully grown cat, in one of the cages looking at me. He was reclining like a lion and had the most unforgettable green eyes. All I could think about was how beautiful he was. A shelter worker placed Bodhidharma on my lap and his heart rested on my hands. The first sensation that I felt was his magnificence and his tenderness. The immediate sense of connection made me cry."

Margaret: "Bodhidharma watches everything that is going on in their apartment from his 'throne' on the kitchen table or from the arm of Anne Marie's wheelchair. He seems to notice everything about Anne Marie: her posture, the rhythm of her breathing, and the slightest changes in her voice. If he senses something is off, he meows loudly until one of her caregivers notices and helps her. Sometimes this means that Anne Marie's throat needs to be cleared. He even sleeps on Anne Marie's chest at night, which brings her comfort and allows him to monitor her breathing while she is sleeping. And their relationship isn't just one-sided. Recently Anne Marie noticed Bodhidharma was drinking more water than usual. This led us to find he had a urinary tract infection that otherwise might not have been detected. At other times, Anne Marie has noticed a mild limp, a change in his grooming frequency, and even a flinching along his back. These signs let us know that Bodhidharma needed chiropractic attention."

Anne Marie: *"Because of my health condition and being restricted in this wheelchair, I feel embarrassed to take up space. But watching Bodhidharma stretch and walk, and be so present without embarrassment or shame, has taught me to feel the joy of being alive in my own body again. Through Bodhidharma's influence, though it's taken me fifty-four years, I've finally come to understand the preciousness of life. He has introduced me to a whole new dimension of love for all animals, which includes humans."*

Margaret: *"The connection between Anne Marie and Bodhidharma is extraordinary; it's as if they can read each other's minds. Their bond of love and dedication to one another surpasses any animal-human connection that I have ever witnessed. It's an honor to be in his presence. His name, Bodhiharma, says it all. He is a high being."*

PEN PALS

"These dogs have caused me to take a long hard look deep within myself. Today, I am a better person than I was before."
—Gilbert, an inmate at San Quentin State Prison

Marin County, California is a short car ride over the Golden Gate Bridge from San Francisco. It is the home to ancient redwoods, the Grateful

Dead, and George Lucas's Skywalker Ranch. It is also the home of San Quentin State Prison and the Marin Humane Society.

What does the state's oldest correctional institution have in common with a dog shelter? Pen Pals.

Pen Pals is a program where inmates at San Quentin care for, socialize, and train rescue dogs before the dogs are returned to the Marin Humane Society for adoption. Larry Carson developed Pen Pals after seeing a television program where dogs were placed with inmates for rehabilitation. The program cut down prison violence by 30 percent. The warden of that prison told Larry it was the best program they had ever had.

The inmates who participate in the Pen Pals program are responsible for exercising, feeding, and giving medications to the dogs. Karen Gulmon, the program coordinator for Pen Pals, told me that the dogs share a room with their assigned inmate. "Lying next to a warm and friendly body who responds to them a positive way can be an invaluable opportunity for an inmate's rehabilitation," she said. These inmates also serve as fire fighters and EMTs for the prison.

I followed Lonnie, one of the Pen Pal inmates, for a tour of the firehouse, where the prisoners and the dogs live together. Lonnie grew up in Louisiana, where, he said, he was used to seeing dogs chained in yards and pitted against each other in fights. Pen Pals, he says, opened his eyes to treating dogs in a different way. "The dogs that come here are shy, needy, and afraid," he told me. "Many have been cruelly treated. You have to earn their trust to help them, and when you do, that's a beautiful feeling. At first, I didn't want to be in the program, but Pen Pals has taught me how to be kinder to dogs." He added, "It goes both ways, you know: I may train them, but they train me back too."

Pen Pals inmates keep daily logs of their activities. The following statements are excerpts from those logs:

> **Buck:** *"I've been with Buck now since June, and we've formed an incredible bond with each other. In times of great distress and sadness, Buck was always able to make me smile. He would do these weird dog things that only a dog named Buck could do. Trivial things he did that no one would think twice about,*

would somehow remind me that everything would be okay. You know, Buck came here to San Quentin to get healthy again, but little did anyone know, that Buck coming here actually made me healthy again too. He got my spirit to be healthy and reminded me that things may not be as bad as they seem. Just depends on how you look at it. Love, affection, and friendship is what Buck can offer you when you adopt him. And he can give you a little bit of something else too. For me it was hope."

Etta: "When Etta first got here, she had a broken leg and was afraid of absolutely everything... car rides, queer noises, hands, even the stairs! Seeing a human being could send her into a shaking fit. She would run into the corner and push herself into the wall like she could pass through it or something. Today, she seeks attention from just about everyone she meets. If something frightens her, like sudden movements, or unfriendly people, she quickly forgives and tries to approach again. I credit one thing to this amazing turn-around. That one thing is love. It's miraculous how just a little bit of genuine love can bring out the absolute best in a fearful dog like Etta. Love can do extraordinary things to us too. Etta's proved that to me."

Twinkie: "By now, I will be long gone but knowing full well that I will still be thinking about Twinkie. I'll always worry about her, that's just the type of person that I am. If you have any trouble with her, it's all my fault. I'm afraid to admit that I spoiled her rotten. I ask that whoever is reading these notes, please take special care of this beautiful dog. She has had enough! She has been hurt too many times. I pray that you are the one to take this heavy weight from her shoulders. Please tell her for me that I have never stopped thinking about her. Twinkie and I did time at San Quentin, bless her heart, she set me right! I'm always missing you, Twinkie."

While at San Quentin, Karen Gulimon, two volunteers, and I sat around a conference table with a handful of inmates, discussing their week with their dogs. Earlier, Karen had told me that in prison, inmates speak with a flat affect and don't show any affection. "It's a survival technique," she said. But when the inmates spoke of "their dogs," their voices told another story.

Pedro shared how caring for Jack, a beagle who was saved from the Korean meat trade, had taught him patience, a quality necessary for raising a child. Eric told us how much laughter the dogs have brought to his life. When I asked Lonnie how the dogs had helped him, his eyes grew thoughtful.

"They've given me a sense of accomplishment," he said. "I feel like I've left my mark in a positive way. They've also taught me tolerance, which I think is the best key in life. I'm not only more tolerant with dogs, but with other humans too. I used to get angry really fast, but I don't anymore. I've learned to let things go, to be more forgiving. These dog moments help us to have more human moments too."

Cats and dogs give so much of themselves for the benefit of their human friends. Can we embrace their model of service and give a little more to each other, whether it is our time, a few extra dollars, or some other form of a helping hand? Even a smile can go a long way to uplift another's day when the world feels at its darkest. By modeling service, animals can guide mankind, and womankind, to become one-of-a-kind.

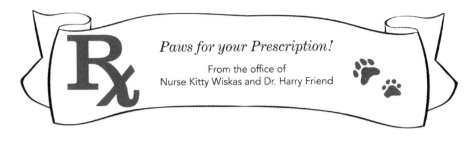

Paws for your Prescription!

From the office of
Nurse Kitty Wiskas and Dr. Harry Friend

1. Do you have an extra hour to give to someone who really needs you? Don't let another week go by; volunteer today!

2. Not sure what kind of service is right for you? What do you love to do? What are you good at? Do you like to be around kids or older people? If it's us that you enjoy best, why not visit your local shelter? We can always use a walk, play time, and affection while we wait for our forever guardians to find us.

3. Shop for service opportunities online. VolunteerMatch. org, Idealist.org, and HandsOnNetwork.org can help you find and contact nonprofits and volunteer organizations that will be a good match for you.

COMING UP: What a ride you've been on! You've journeyed beyond your comfort zone and written a new song about your cat, and today you showed up to the shelter and surrendered yourself to love. Can you feel your extraordinary spirit soaring just a little bit? Turn the page and you will fly even higher!

CHAPTER 19

The Freedom in Forgiveness

"To err is human—to forgive, canine."

—Unknown

I grew up in a Latino family that loved to laugh. I learned about strength, courage, and the importance of hard work from my parents, who displayed all of these qualities throughout their lives, even in the face of great adversity and loss. I also learned another behavior, one at which I excelled: holding a grudge.

As a child, I often felt trapped by my well-meaning parents, who I felt regulated my every move. I was a child who longed to be an adult, to have charge of my own life, and to make my own decisions. I don't use the word "hate" very often, but I sure hated the feeling of being controlled by other people.

Growing up, I watched adults hold grudges against neighbors, friends, and even their own family members. I quickly realized that harboring a grudge was something that no one but me could control, and I liked that very much—so I began to hold grudges of my own, and I became really, really good at it. No matter how much I was limited by authority figures or how much my own voice was subverted, I could conjure up my anger and her cousin, blame, and pack them all around my heart like concrete. It was a power no one could take away from me.

This attitude followed me into adulthood and into a string of failed relationships. It would be many years before I found that the key to freedom lay in something I'd never really tried before: forgiveness.

EXPLORING FORGIVENESS

There is a pleasant righteousness in holding a grudge and refusing to forgive . . . initially. But once time passes and that early surge of adrenaline subsides, it takes lots of energy to hold on to those negative feelings. We may think we want an apology, financial retribution, or vindication, but if we are honest with ourselves, what we really want is more likely kindness, understanding, and empathy for our wounds. When we don't get those things, the resentment we feel can transform into a quiet rage, and like a slow-acting poison, it can spread through your whole body.

According to research by Dr. Michael Barry, author of *The Forgiveness Project*, "The anger and hatred that comes from harboring negative emotions creates a state of chronic anxiety."[97] In my case, the poison eventually found a home in my spine. For twenty years I dealt with debilitating back spasms that doctors could not explain the cause of. The pain was so intense that even taking shallow breaths felt excruciating.

No two people look at the world in the same way. Our individual life experiences, varied cultures, and different levels of education are some of the factors that contribute to our diverse perspectives. Unfortunately, divergent points of view are often the beginning of disagreement, hard feelings, and criticism—all of which can lead to resentment and the inability to forgive.

If you are holding on to negative emotions toward someone else, and you feel justified in doing so, you may wonder if forgiving them will make you seem weak or like a pushover. It doesn't. In *The How of Happiness*, author Sonja Lyubomirsky tells us that forgiveness is not about denying what has happened or condoning what someone else has done. Forgiveness is acknowledging what has happened, feeling your emotions, and deciding how you want to look at it in the future.

YOUR GET-OUT-OF-JAIL-FREE CARD

Take a moment to close your eyes and ask yourself, *Who or what situation do I need to forgive?* What is the first thing that comes to mind? What do you feel in your body when you think of that person or event? Is there a heavy weight in your chest, tension around your shoulders, or does your head begin to ache? How would you rather feel? How much better would your life be if you could drop the weight of blame?

There is a powerful link between forgiveness and your well-being. The following is a short list of some of the benefits to your mind, body, and spirit.

THE GIFTS IN FORGIVING

- Reduces stress
- Improves heart health
- Decreases anxiety
- Increases self-esteem
- Improves relationships
- Creates a positive role model for children
- Greater sense of freedom

If you have been holding on to a past grievance and are finding it hard to let bygones be bygones, your cats and dogs can provide a judgment-free, safe, and loving environment as you brave the process of forgiveness. By licking our emotional wounds, forgiving our own failings, and cherishing us (even when we can't do that for ourselves), our animals provide us with a priceless blanket of support.

Tom learned how life-changing forgiveness can be from Jackie, an unexpected guest who came to stay.

Jackie & Tom

"Schweinhund"—"Pig Dog"—that's what they called her. No wonder she kept turning up at our house.

She sat patiently on the porch, just beyond the screen door, occasionally looking in. She was a fine-looking creature, trim and athletic—a Belgian Malinois, we later learned. She had no collar, so we put one on her and taped our phone number to it. We adored her for a week, and then one day she disappeared.

The next day, we got a call: "Our dog, Schweinhund"—he uttered the word like a foul expulsion—"she has a collar with your phone number on it."

"Yes," I said, "she didn't have any ID, so we put it on. You know, in case she got lost?"

"Well, she is ours."

"Uh, okay. But, she should have a collar. And has she had her shots? Is she spayed?"

"Yeah, we're working on all that."

Father and son came to take her back. But a week later she was back on our porch wearing our old collar, the taped phone number removed and nothing else added. I called the Schweinmeister.

"Hi, this is Tom from down the street."

"Oh. She is back with you?"

"Yes. And I'm thinking she'll just stay with us. I mean, I still don't see any ID, or license, no tags. Nothing. And . . . it's . . . it's just not cool. People have a responsibility when they care for animals; don't you think?"

We renamed her Jackie when she came to live with us. At the time, "us" was my wife, Mary, our two daughters, Ava (10) and Laura (7), and me, and her arrival came at an uneasy time of life; seven years prior, I'd left a cushy job in LA in order to try and make an independent feature film in New Mexico. The effort had drained our money and strained my marriage. I didn't know it at the time, but my wife and I were a year away from separation. Stress was high in our home, and patience was low. I shouted a lot, mostly at Jackie.

"No!"

"Outside, I said!"

"Now!"

My epiphany came when Jackie gave me a deliberate side-look just before she nosed open the back door one day. Her look said, "Geez, dude. Chill. I am not the problem. Maybe it's you."

And it was. Time stopped, and I shrank in shame. What the hell am I doing? I wondered. Why am I yelling so much? I was blindly and defensively transforming my hurt into anger and projecting it onto the ones I loved: my children, my wife, and poor Jackie.

That incident led me to a recognition, and as quickly and thoroughly as I could, I changed my behavior. Admittedly, decades later, the reversal is still not complete; the work is ongoing. But I've gotten a lot better.

I learned another, related lesson from Jackie as well. Throughout those dark times, she never seemed to hold a grudge; all was forgiven no matter what I'd done, and every moment was new. I felt the value in that. When combined with a new awareness of my faults, it precipitated a kind of freedom—a weightlessness resulting from the release of the past and its baggage.

Yes, Jackie took things as they came, and I'm ever grateful to follow her lead. If I could put into words what I learned from her, it's acceptance. I'm reminded of Reinhold Niebuhr's Serenity Prayer:

"God, grant me the serenity to accept the things I cannot change,

The courage to change the things I can,

And the wisdom to know the difference."

These days (thank you, Jackie), I rarely worry about the things I cannot change.

As you now know, being forgiving is not a quality that has come to me naturally, But thanks to moments like the following one, I am frequently reminded of the power and importance of forgiveness, often by my cats and dogs—like Jester and Rudy, for instance.

Jester, Rudy & Carlyn

Cats are all extraordinary, but my black-and-white tuxedo cat, Jester, was truly a sage. Now that he has passed, my heart still feels his presence. Perhaps it's his fur that I continue to find around the house, even though it's been months since we said good-bye; or the faint jingle of a bell, which makes my heart leap with the thought that in a moment he will be rounding the corner.

Jester died quite unexpectedly, and when he left, he took an irreplaceable piece of my heart with him. In its place, however, he left a precious gift: a moment of forgiveness that will remain with me forever.

Months before Jester passed away, the strangest thing occurred. He and Rudy, my chocolate lab mix, suddenly, unexplainably, and violently began to fight. I threw myself into the melee, adrenaline racing through my veins, blocking out the pain of the accruing scratches on my arms.

Finally I managed to separate Rudy and Jester. I wasn't as worried about Rudy, who outweighed Jester by forty pounds. Instead, my heart went out to my little cat, who, as soon as he was freed from the corner he was backed up against, jetted up the stairs, leaving a tiny trail of blood behind him.

After a careful inspection of both cat and dog bodies, I sighed with relief. Jester had suffered a couple of injured nails, which the vet said would heal on their own. Rudy had a small puncture on his face, but we kept it clean and fortunately it never became infected.

The greater damage appeared to be not physical but emotional. I'd always kidded my husband that Jester thought he was a dog. Jester loved to lie with the dogs as they sunned themselves in front of our cathedral windows or nestle next to them on their beds for a movie-watching session in the evenings. Whereas Cody, my yellow tabby, tolerated the dogs, Jester wanted to be their friend. Until that day, he and Rudy had been just that. But now they were mistrustful of each other.

Following the fight, Jester spent a lot of time in the closet or cuddled next to me on the bed, as if seeking protection. Rudy, on the other hand, would lower his eyes and slink away every time Jester entered the room.

A month passed, and although we became accustomed to the new dynamic, it broke my heart to see the crevasse that had developed between my two animal friends.

One morning, Ken and I were mid-conversation when we saw the most remarkable thing: Rudy was standing in the kitchen, and Jester was sitting about a foot away, facing him. They had not been this physically close since their skirmish. Today there was no tension between them, no wariness; just a curiosity as they looked into one another's eyes. We watched, intrigued by the wordless communication taking place in front of us. Moments passed, each one feeling like an eternity. Then, as if a phone line had suddenly been severed, the energy shifted between them. Jester stepped towards Rudy and stretched his neck toward his face, touching his tiny nose to the tip of Rudy's big red snout.

There are times in life when you feel a connection to more than your-self; to more than your small life; as if you are connected to the heartbeat of the world. This was one of those times. Rudy and Jester held their powerful touch for a few brief seconds, and then it was over; the moment was gone, and each went their own way. But in that moment, forgiveness had been offered and accepted. My boys were friends again.

There is a Hawaiian prayer called the Ho'oponopono. It is a prayer of forgiveness, and it goes like this:

I am sorry
Please forgive me
I love you
Thank you

The Ho'oponopono prayer uses powerful words—sorry, forgive, love and thanks. It is a potent way to set things right within ourselves when we feel someone has hurt us. It's one thing to decide never to play with people who have hurt us again. That can be a sign that we are practicing healthy boundaries. But when we fortify our lack of forgive-ness, we are just as much prisoners of our state of mind as the person we choose not to forgive. Embracing forgiveness is the key to freedom, happiness, and wellness.

Perhaps Jester and Rudy shared their own interspecies version of the Ho'oponopono with each other. Ultimately, I will never know what was communicated between them, but in that moment, I saw the enormous power that comes with forgiveness. Forgive everything, forgive everyone, and—maybe most of all—forgive yourself. That's what Jester and Rudy taught me.

Paws for your Prescription!

From the office of
Nurse Kitty Wiskas and Dr. Harry Friend

1. Who can you forgive today? Is it a past lover, a parent, or is it yourself? It takes a little courage to forgive. When you need some, borrow a little bit of ours.

2. Say the Ho'oponopono during your morning ritual and you will see just how much brighter your and our day can become.

3. Have you ever seen dogs dig a hole? We dig and dig and dig until we find the bone we are looking for! Forgiveness is a similar process. You have to dig a little every day until you finally reach the bones in your heart; then you can chew 'em up and toss 'em out.

COMING UP: To let your extraordinary spirit continue to soar, you must be willing to surrender, even to what may be your greatest fear . . .

CHAPTER 20

The Art of Living with Dying

*"If there are no dogs in heaven, then when I die
I want to go where they went."*

—Will Rogers

When I was a kid, death did not visit often. I would hear my parents speak in hushed whispers about remote family members who had died, but none were close enough to my heart to elicit any emotion. At a certain point, with a child's naiveté, I began to wonder if my family was immune to such tragedies.

When my grandmother died in my early twenties, I didn't see my mother cry. After the funeral I watched her in the kitchen stirring a pot on the stove, and wondered if she felt anything. Today, I know my mother experienced tremendous grief when her mother passed, but she viewed crying as a weakness and stoicism as strength; at the time, though, it seemed that death simply didn't affect her.

It wasn't until I was in my forties that death finally hit home, and when it did, it hit hard, as if making up for lost time. First my mother died; then, a few years later, a rare blood disease took my nephew's life. In quick succession, my father, father-in-law, sister, and mother-in-law also passed away.

Different cultures respond to death's arrival in distinct ways. Dr. Therese A. Rando, PhD, says there are three patterns that describe how societies respond to death: *death-defying, death-accepting,* and *death-denying.* Death-defying cultures, the ancient Egyptians for example, sought to thwart death by having their possessions and even their loved ones buried with them when they went. *Death-accepting cultures,* like the Fiji Islanders, employ mourning rituals to help them accept the dying process with greater ease. But in western cultures, like we have in the US, we have more difficulty accepting death. For us, death is perhaps the most earth-shattering and fear-inducing experience we face in our lifetime. According to Dr. Rando, we are a *death-denying* culture.[98]

Whether you are a billionaire or a gardener, you will meet death many times over in your life, from the loss of your loved ones to your own passing. You may feel that you have no control over death, but what you do have power over is the view you take of the experience. Death can be the monster in your closet or an unexpected opportunity for growth.

In her book *The Top Five Regrets of the Dying: A Life Transformed by the Dearly Departing,* Bronnie Ware, an Australian nurse who spent years caring for people in the last months of their lives, explains what most people wish for at the end of their days. She says that there are five things she heard again and again from people whose time was up:

I WISH . . .

1. I had the courage to live a life true to myself.
2. I hadn't worked so hard.
3. I had the courage to express my feelings.
4. I had stayed in touch with my friends.
5. I had let myself be happier.[99]

If this were your last day on earth, what would you wish for? Would you prefer to arrive at the end of your journey with less regret and a greater sense of wonder? What if your fear could be tempered by acceptance and your sadness lessened by hope? If the five statements above reflect your own wishes, your animal friends are the genies in the bottle that can help make them come true.

WHAT DOGS & CATS TEACH US ABOUT *LIVING* WITH THE END

Does a day go by when your cat or dog doesn't make you laugh? Can more than a couple of hours pass before a wet nudge reminds you it's time to connect by scratching a furry head or if they allow it, offering a gentle kiss? These are the ways our cats and dogs help us to live with death—by reminding us that the important moments in *life* are often those that are small, brief, and ultimately precious.

Animals are who they are; your cat doesn't think she's a lion, and your dachshund would never consider himself a poodle. By modeling how to live authentically, our cats and dogs offer us an opportunity to remember to do the same. And a life genuinely lived gives us the strength to meet our final days with the same authenticity.

We all want our beloved animal friends to live forever, but only our cats have nine lives. And because cat and dog lives are so much shorter than ours, we animal lovers have to say good-bye to many four-legged family members over the years.

I've heard many people say that the pain of losing their cat or dog is too much to bear, and for this reason, they've decided never to adopt another animal again. My heart breaks when I hear this. There are millions of cats and dogs—similar to the one you loved—who are wasting away in shelters and on the streets. One of these dog doctors or cat nurses could add so much to your health and happiness. Choosing to love again can not only heal your broken heart, it can also save an animal's life. Animals feel loss, they grieve, and they also move on. Their culture is one of death acceptance. I doubt they would want their beloved guardians to mourn them forever.

As children, losing our animal friends may be the first loss we ever experience. As adults, it doesn't get any easier to go through this struggle. But even as we say good-bye with tears, we're being given a chance to learn that death is a natural part of our life cycle.

Saying good-bye is the price we pay for loving and being loved in return. And for those of us who have loved and loved hard, we know that love never dies, as long as its memory finds a home in the heart. For proof of this, just look to Beth's story about her son, Max, and how a crazy dog named Leo arrived into her life at a time when she needed him the most.

Leo, Max & Beth

When my son Max turned eighteen, he brought a seventy-pound brindled pit bull home to live with us. Since I was a child, I'd had a phobia around pit bulls, so I made Leo sleep in the car for three nights before I ever let him in the house. When I did finally let him through the front door, I discovered he was a crazy dog who chewed up everything—TV remotes, cell phones, eyeglass cases, you name it.

I thought Leo was aggressive until the first time Max's girlfriend brought over her Chihuahua, Mimi. Mimi jumped up and down and barked at Leo whenever he tried to come into the bedroom. Leo, as big as he was, shook in the doorway, frightened of a tiny dog.

Max was a wonderful, creative, and kind young man. He was an expert at martial arts, an artist, a break-dancer, and a rapper. But on August 31, 2014, Max was shot and killed by two armed men during a robbery. The men were apprehended, found guilty, and given long prison sentences.

It was hard for people to understand what it was like to lose a child. My friends and family had trouble understanding that with Max gone, my life had changed forever. Day to day I was making the motions of going through this strange reality, the new normal that had become my existence without Max. I had moments of being able to function, but not a lot of them. I had to keep asking my friends to help me with the simplest things, like putting my taxes in an envelope or cleaning my house. These were easy things that I had done all of my life, but now I couldn't motivate myself to do any of them.

With Max gone, Leo was a handful to deal with. But Max had loved him so much that I could not send him away.

I would put Leo in my truck and we'd drive to the Russian River, where I had grown up and where my cabin was. While driving I'd think of Max and hear his beautiful laugh in my mind. I'd miss him so much that I would start crying. Leo would put his paw on me like he was trying to help me drive. His presence would calm me and the look on his face would make me laugh.

I didn't want Leo at first, but over time things began to change. When I was having a rough day, I couldn't wait to get home to him, because he was always so happy to see me. I'd crawl into bed with him and we would get under the covers, where it was nice and toasty, and as we lay there together, I'd remember how when Max was alive, he'd come into my room and give me a kiss. Leo would be lying on the bed next to me, and Max would lie down beside us and hug and kiss Leo too. Max and Leo were so alike; both were large, exuberant, energetic, and affectionate. Those are beautiful memories for me.

I now see how dogs can be such an important part of a person's healing process. When you are grieving, they are there for you, body and soul. I may have not wanted Leo in the beginning, but now I never want to be away from him. Caring for Leo has kept me going. He has shown me how to slow down, and to appreciate the little things in life, like a long walk along the river. If I didn't have Leo I'd probably be rocking back and forth in a corner somewhere. Recently, I quit my job as a schoolteacher, and now I get to spend a lot more time with him.

The worst thing in life that you could ever experience is to lose your son. I miss him every moment of every day. But Leo is the greatest gift Max could have left me. Leo is my doctor, my nurse, my friend, and my refuge. He's better than antidepressants, alcohol, or any of the other things you might turn to when you lose a child. Our moments together have saved me. Max left me a crazy and wonderful dog, and for that I'm forever grateful.

AND THEN THERE WERE TWO

When I decided to write this book, I didn't know it would take me five years to complete it. I also never considered that during that time I would have to say good-bye to so many that I loved.

When this book was still just a concept, a friend of mine recommended that I see an Intuitive for a psychic reading. Terry the Intuitive was a kind fellow who put me at ease with his pleasant manner and gentle voice. As we sat in his garden and drank herbal tea, I told him that I wanted to write a book about how cats and dogs help enhance human health. Terry looked up from his teacup, an odd expression on his face, and said one word to me: "Hurry!"

A year later, Teddy, my sixteen-year-old black chow, died. As I held him close to me and kissed him one last time, I remembered what Terry the Intuitive had said. The following year, when Cody, my beautiful golden tabby, died of lung cancer, I again heard the echo of Terry's *"Hurry!"* A month later, when Roxy suddenly became ill, I began to realize what Terry had meant.

When Roxy got sick, the doctors ran a myriad of tests to determine her unexplained condition. For three days I lived on a futon next to her enclosure at the animal emergency hospital. If I left Roxy alone, even to go to the bathroom, she would let out a series of high-pitched, distressed yips. So I lay beside her, stroking her coat, whispering gently into her ear, hoping for both of us.

When the doctor told me she suspected Roxy had cancer, and that it might not be treatable, I reacted like I've always reacted to bad news: without reaction. I stared at the back of the doctor's lab coat well after she was no longer there, trying to wrap my head around her words.

Just then, I realized Roxy was staring at me. Perhaps my heart knew what my mind was not willing to admit, because as I gazed into her fawn-like eyes, my heart began to tear open. As tears clouded my vision, I felt Roxy's imminent loss, as well as the other losses that hadn't made their way out of my system yet. I cried for Teddy, for Cody, for my mother, for my father, and even for myself. *How will I survive without those I love?* I wondered. *How does one endure these repeated blows to the heart?*

I couldn't bear the rawness of my emotions, and I turned away from Roxy's gaze. She sighed loudly and put her head down next to me as I cried myself to sleep, repeating these questions over and over in my mind until they were lost in my dreams.

When I woke up, a tech was checking Roxy's vitals. As I watched her jot notes on a chart, Roxy's paw touched my hand, just like the first time she got my attention in the shelter where I had found her. That touch brought me the answer I was looking for, and three words sounded in my head: "Find the meaning."

Because of Roxy's behavioral challenges, I learned how to help her move through some old layers of anxiety and fear, and in the process, I'd had to do some emotional housecleaning of my own. Over time, a happier and more authentic version of myself was the result. Roxy's companionship had taught me some priceless lessons. And now she was teaching me my greatest lesson of all: how to live with death by finding greater and deeper meaning in my life's experiences, including the loss of those I loved.

Each day, after he got off work, Ken came to visit Roxy and bring me dinner. On this day, she yipped at him and licked his hand, and a few minutes later she suffered a stroke and died in my arms. It was as if she had been waiting for the three of us to be together again before saying good-bye.

The morning after Roxy passed over, I stepped out of the veterinary clinic and watched as a quiet breeze moved through the purple, pink, and white primroses that had yet to be trampled by dog paws. The vibrant colors of these flowers reminded me of a rainbow. This connection made my mind wander to a poem I once heard about a rainbow bridge:

> *There is a place connecting heaven and earth*
> *called the Rainbow Bridge,*
> *where animals go once we leave this life.*
> *There are meadows and hills, sunshine and food.*
> *We wait there to be reunited with our Guardian friends*
> *and once we are, we cross over that bridge together,*
> *never to be separated again.*[100]

My dog was gone, but she wasn't dead, and in that moment I knew I would one day be with her again.

Paws for your Prescription!

From the office of
Nurse Kitty Wiskas and Dr. Harry Friend

1. Saying good-bye to someone you love is sad and confusing. As your best friends, we are here to comfort, support, and love you until you are ready to smile again.

2. If your young child is having a hard time coping with loss, and they don't want to talk to anyone else, encourage them to talk to us. We're good listeners.

3. If your grief is lasting a long time, please seek out an expert. You may be surprised to find one of us working in the office alongside them.

COMING UP: Do you believe in life after death? If not, keep reading. If so, keep reading. The tao of dog and the way of the cat awaits you on the other side . . . of the page.

CHAPTER 21

The Tao of Dog, The Way of Cat

"All beings are much more similar than they are different.
We should be looking for the connection between ourselves, and
our animal friends, instead of what sets us apart.
This is how we come to discover our humanity."

—Jane Goodall

The healthy spirit is the final piece of the trifecta of mind, body, and spirit that leads to an extraordinary life—and it may be the most important piece. Allowing our spirits to soar requires nurturing our consciousness.

Like love, consciousness is difficult to define, and even the greatest minds have struggled with this challenge. But here's what we do know: Consciousness is the state of how we perceive reality and interpret our experiences. For example, we are *conscious* of the red balloon in a child's hand, the icy cold when we step into the snow, and the anger we feel when slighted by a loved one.

What this chapter focuses on is our *higher consciousness*—the aspect of our spirit that is unique to each of us and transcends our physical senses. This higher self houses our unlimited, unbridled, and undying potential.

In the last twenty chapters, you've read much about how cats and dogs model a number of attributes that contribute to a healthier and happier life. Good nutrition, encouraging exercise, nurturing positive thoughts and words, helping us build relationships, and even demonstrating the art of living with dying are some of the ways that our friends offer us daily opportunities to follow their lead and enhance our well-being.

Our companions' influence does not have to stop here. If we believe our animal friends to be our copilots on our life's journey, our kinship with them can inspire our self-transformation in an even bigger way—three ways, to be exact. They can guide us toward experiencing a higher consciousness with each other, with the natural world, and even beyond this existence.

1. CONSCIOUSNESS WITH EACH OTHER

We all know how it feels when someone walks into a room and the energy shifts. If that person is consistently griping about their boss or complaining about their girlfriend, we want to get away from them post-haste. Worse, if the chip falls off their shoulder and onto ours, it becomes us who people are fleeing away from.

But when the opposite happens and the person who enters the room is laughing even though they just got drenched in a rain shower or they offer their coworker a congratulatory hug even though they got passed over for the promotion, *this* is the person we all want to be near. Clearly, how we feel affects those around us, even when we don't utter a single word.

After my divorce, I literally had to force myself out of bed and drag myself to the editing rooms of whatever film I was working on. Once there, I didn't want to engage with anyone. My negative vibe didn't exactly make my workmates flock to say "good morning" to me, either.

Things changed when I met Ken. It was love at first sight, and the power of our connection was life-changing. I began sleeping more soundly, I received a promotion at work, and my coworkers began smiling at me instead of running for cover. Falling in love altered my perception of the world. It shifted my consciousness.

Dr. Deepak Chopra, author and alternative medicine advocate, says, "When you have the experience of love, either giving it or receiving it, you become magnanimous to the rest of the world. That's why people in love can do extraordinary things!"[101] We may not be able to sustain being *in* love 100 percent of the time, but often all that keeps us from moving in that direction (i.e., toward a higher conscious state) is making the choice to do so. Of course, when our minds are stuck in negative thought loops, it's hard to imagine breaking free of them, much less feeling love. Sometimes we need a little nudge to get us moving down the right path again. Our animal friends are great candidates to help us reset our bad vibes into good ones and begin making our way toward love again.

Showing kindness, finding compassion, and giving love to someone you may not even like is a tough nut for most humans to crack. But before you give up, try this cat- and dog-inspired exercise:

THE CAT & DOG LOVER'S TRICK TO LIKING HUMANS

- Take three deep breaths
- Imagine the person you dislike in your mind's eye.
- Take three more deep breaths
- Now, imagine that person as . . . *a cat or dog.*
- Take three more deep breaths—or laugh. Whichever comes first.

For example, when I get mad at my husband, who is a gentle and kind human being (except when I'm angry with him, of course), I imagine him as a playful beagle. When the girl in the Mini Cooper cuts me off on the freeway because she is busy applying her lipstick in her rearview mirror, I think, *frisky feline.* And when the salesperson over the phone is testing my patience, I envision a lab with floppy ears.

Call me crazy, but this little trick brings an immediate smile to my face. As an animal lover, I have never met a cat or dog I didn't like; so when I think of a person as one of these furry friends, it becomes much harder for me not to like that person. The moment of levity is enough to keep my thoughts from spiraling down a negative path and allows me some breathing room to choose more positive, patient, and empowered thoughts.

Thanks to my dog doctors and cat nurses, the next person I run into will see a smiling face instead of a frowning one. Hopefully, that smile will be contagious enough to share with others. After all, a smiling world is always a better one.

2. CONSCIOUSNESS WITH NATURE

One of the primary differences between traditional Chinese medicine (TCM) and western medicine is that in TCM we treat the *whole person*, not just their affected parts. For example, if you are a guitar player with arthritis in your wrist from overuse, an acupuncturist will help relieve that pain, but they will also be interested in the dark circles under your eyes, the purple tinge of your tongue, and the crease forming on your ear lobe. These signs may seem unrelated, but they are important clues to your overall health.

If you can believe that you are not just random body parts but rather part of a whole and connected body, then you may be willing to take it one step further and realize that you are part of an even greater whole. Each of us is a microcosm of a much larger macrocosm. We are connected to our environment, our planet, and even the universe in more ways than we might imagine. This interconnectedness with our natural world is a vital part of our well-being.

The famous astronomer Carl Sagan revealed that all life on earth—trees, dogs, cats, and human beings—comes from the stars. This means that we are all made of the same atomic particles, all made of the same matter. Technically, we are all made of stardust.

Our growing urban landscapes, expanding technologies, and insulated existence move us away from nature and her healing powers. For this we pay a heavy price. One need only look at the ecological chaos around us now, such as the destruction of the rainforest, the disappearance of the honeybees, and the infiltration of GMO crops, to see that the list of ways we are sacrificing our world and ourselves is growing at a frightening pace.

We may be apathetic to, or just unaware of, our disconnectedness from nature, but our animal companions have not forgotten this connection. Cats and dogs are nature's gatekeepers and her representatives in our homes, gentle reminders that nature is ever present and waiting for humans to wake up to this connection.

Throughout your day, take notice of the gentle prods your cats and dogs give you. They know when you need to take a break and disengage from your busy life. Watching the sunset with your cat on your lap, going for a moonlit walk on the beach with your dog, taking a nap in the sunshine with both . . . these are the quiet moments that can help us shift our consciousness and reconnect to the nature of all things.

3. CONSCIOUSNESS AND BEYOND

Along with Pope Francis and Robert Redford, Dr. Robert Lanza, an expert in stem cell science, has been considered by *Time Magazine* to be one of the one hundred most influential people in the world.[102] Dr. Lanza has been lauded by astrophysicists and Nobel Prize winners. He is also the coauthor of *Biocentrism: How Life and Consciousness are the Keys to Understanding the True Nature of the Universe.*

In this groundbreaking book, Dr. Lanza explains how our consciousness is what creates the material world around us. He also proposes that although our bodies cease to function at death, the mathematical possibility of our consciousness ending at that time is zero. Consciousness, he says, exists beyond time and space; your body may die, but your awareness goes on forever.[103]

If, as Dr. Lanza suggests, consciousness is what survives in each of us even after we die, then should it not follow that our consciousness is the number one thing we should be nurturing while we're alive?

Even if you believe that life ends with the death of your physical body, doesn't fostering consciousness during your lifetime still make the best sense? Savoring moments with our loved ones, exploring creativity, finding time to play, and enjoying nature—these are just a few of the countless ways our animal companions help us cultivate our own consciousness and make our life experience that much more extraordinary.

Much has been said about cats and their nine lives, but what about a kitty's consciousness? This was a question that Cindy, a die-hard dog lover, came face to face with a few years ago.

Toulouse, Spider & Cindy

Our dog, Pookie, was a cute beagle-terrier mix who we'd had since she was six weeks old. My husband and I were dog people through and through, and had never really understood anything about cats.

Two young cat brothers, Spider and Toulouse, lived next door to us. Every day we'd see them sitting on the top of the fence between our houses, where they would watch Pookie zip around the yard. Pookie would bark and sometimes playfully chase after them if they jumped down. As often as they played with Pookie, however, they always kept their distance from us.

When Pookie was sixteen, she died in my arms. She was old, and had lived a great life with us. Even so, I was heartbroken to lose her. I didn't realize at the time that help was on the way.

Early the next morning, as if it happened every day, Toulouse and Spider jumped down from the fence and walked straight into our house. They did the same thing the next day, and then the next. I was sitting on the couch thinking of Pookie one afternoon when Toulouse jumped on my lap, and his purring and warmth helped comfort me. It was if both he and Spider knew how much we'd loved our dog, and they were letting us know that everything was going to be all right.

Technically, Toulouse and Spider belonged to our neighbors, and in particular their daughter, a little girl named Finn. But over the years these orange tabbies began to spend their days mostly with us. Eventually our home began to fill with cat beds, food bowls, and a variety of toys.

Toulouse, named after Henri de Toulouse-Lautrec, the French impressionist artist, was the smaller of the two brothers. He was the sweetest, most lovable, precious kitty. He loved to snuggle and sleep next to my cheek. Toulouse was like an angel on earth.

One day, when Toulouse was in the yard, some teenagers drove by and shot him with a pellet gun. The wound caused nerve damage, leaving him with a permanent limp. Fortunately, Toulouse had a staunch ally in his brother, Spider, who was larger and tougher and would come to Toulouse's defense whenever he saw other cats bullying his little brother.

Years passed, and then the unimaginable happened: Toulouse got hit by a car and died. Maybe even more than when Pookie passed away, I felt devastated. I would look at Toulouse's food bowl and cry uncontrollably. I cried for a week. I'd never realized anyone could cry as much as that over a cat.

Spider was devastated as well. He went into a deep depression, lost weight, and even began to pull out his own fur because of the stress. It was a sad time for all of us.

When my son was very young, I had downloaded an app to my cell phone called Talking Ginger, which was basically just a cat that talked to you over the phone. I hadn't used it in years and had forgotten all about it. Two days after Toulouse died, I was sitting around feeling sad when all of a sudden I heard singing coming from my phone. I picked it up and saw it was an orange tabby with angel wings on the screen. Below the image it said, "I'm a hairy angel now!"

I nearly dropped the phone. I never got notifications from that app, and I have not received another one since that day.

That night when Finn came home, I ran out to show her the picture and said, "Look, it's from Toulouse!"

Finn had been so sad before this, but now a smile covered her face.

After Pookie died, Toulouse and Spider became like my nurses, soothing not only me but my whole family. As they helped me get over my sadness, I got to see cats for the amazing creatures they are. Cats have souls just like ours. They communicate, they love, and they have empathy and compassion. I believe the app going off was a sign from the other side; I think it was Toulouse saying, "I'm okay now, don't worry about me. And thank you for taking such good care of me."

Today, Spider and I have become even more bonded. He always wants to sleep with me and have our bodies touch. He may scratch everyone else, but he lets me kiss him on the nose. We weren't cat people before this, but because of Toulouse and Spider, our eyes are now fully open. Not only are cats smart, wonderful, and loving creatures, they can also communicate with us from the other side. Love has no boundaries.

When someone you love dies, it can feel impossible to say good-bye. But sometimes you get unexpected help from the most unlikely of friends, as Linda did from Kona Bean.

Kona Bean, Susie & Linda

Susie and I had been together for fourteen wonderful years when she was diagnosed with breast cancer. Five years later, she passed away.

Susie died on a Thursday, and because the crematorium was closed until Monday, I was told I could keep Susie's body at home until then. We had Susie's wake in our living room, and in the days that followed, friends dropped by to share their memories and tell stories about her. Our sweet friend Danny crafted a beautiful maple box for Susie to lie in. On the outside, people wrote their messages of love and painted pictures.

One night, Susie's daughter, Mary Beth, her cousin, Kate, and our friends Brook and Marti came by. Everyone added special things inside Susie's box, including some of her favorite chocolate bars—Susie loved her chocolate. She also loved her dogs. Her whippets were part of the family, and extremely important to her. First we had Benjamin, who had passed away a few years before, and now Rosie and Kona Bean were living with us. Susie loved taking them to a big field where she would toss the Frisbee across the grass. Rosie and Kona Bean would give chase, catch the Frisbee in midair, and then bring it back to Susie.

Early Monday morning, I sat in my reading chair watching Susie. Her body was surrounded by flowers and five hundred cards that friends and family had sent us while she was sick. She looked so angelic lying there. I had been up most of the night thinking about our nineteen years together, all of the wonder we had experienced, and how much I had grown as a person because of her. I couldn't bring myself to put the lid on the box and cover her face forever. I wasn't ready to say good-bye, and I told her so out loud.

"How am I going to let you go?" I said. "How am I going to do this?"

No one answered back . . . at first. Then I heard Kona Bean get off her bed. I thought she was going outside to do her morning duty, but instead she came into the room with Susie and me.

"Good morning, Kona," I said.

Kona ignored me and went right up to the maple box, then circled around it. I thought she wanted the chocolate we had put inside, but instead, she put her snout into the box and started flipping over the flowers and cards until Susie's face was completely covered by them. She turned and looked at me, then went straight back to bed.

I sat there in complete amazement. Had Kona heard me talking to Susie? Had Susie told Kona to help me out? I'll never know, but Kona helped me do something I couldn't do on my own: she showed me how to say good-bye to Susie and move on. It was if she was telling me, "The best way to get through this, Linda, is just to do it!"

That moment changed me forever. I felt full of love for Kona, for Susie, and for life. I had never been a dog person like Susie was. I grew up on a farm, and we never treated animals like they were smart. In this one life-changing instance, I was given a huge gift—a realization that animals have more to offer us than we might think. I had promised Susie I would take care of her dogs, but now felt a greater respect, and thankfulness, for Kona. I wondered if this was Susie's way of influencing me to have a greater understanding of and compassion for all animals.

Three months after Susie died, Rosie, our other whippet, came down with cancer and passed away, leaving just Kona Bean and me behind.

When Kona was nearly seventeen, I went to see an animal communicator. The communicator didn't know anything about Kona or me, except that I needed help understanding what Kona wanted in this phase of her life. The communicator said to me, "Well, I can tell you what Kona is thinking, but first I want to say there is a woman here with two dogs. They are on a grassy field and she is throwing a Frisbee for them. She wants you to know they are okay."

Life is a mystery. But because of moments like the one with that communicator, I look at life differently now; I've become kinder, less judgmental, and even happier. I believe life is a journey, and that we are here to do the best we can. Now, I also believe in life after death. When I get caught up in life's challenges and my thoughts, I remember this story, and I ask Susie for help. I know I will see Susie and Kona again; I'll see everybody again. Because of that, I don't have a fear of dying anymore.

When my old chow chow Teddy died, I carried the heaviness of his loss inside me. But what I soon learned was that although he was gone physically, our connection to each other would prove stronger than this life.

Teddy & Carlyn

Three months after Teddy died, I found myself at my favorite restaurant ordering takeout. A tarot card reader with striking green eyes and a felt hat was sitting nearby, offering people free readings. As I waited for my food, I walked over to her table and took her up on her offer.

The reader told me to pick a card out of her deck; when I did, she looked at it and then gave me a generic and unmemorable reading. I thanked her and began to walk away—but just then, a flash of heat moved through my body, from the bottom of my feet into my face, and at the same time I heard the word TEDDY loudly in my mind.

It's taken me a lifetime to not be afraid to listen when my inner guidance speaks to me, so I turned around and told the green-eyed woman with the felt hat about the heat sensation. She nodded and told me we should do a second reading, and this time, both of us should pick a card out of the deck.

After picking our respective cards she looked at each and said, "That's odd, we both picked cards with dogs in them."

I hadn't told her Teddy was a dog.

She then told me she was seeing an image of a black dog against a star-filled sky. Her words made me sit down. I also hadn't told her Teddy was black or that just a week before, my friend Linda had climbed Mount Shasta and brought a small prayer flag with Teddy's name on it to put on the mountain. I remembered Linda describing the night's sky on Mount Shasta as having the most amazing stars she had ever seen. I didn't tell Linda at the time, but after Teddy died, I kept seeing him against a star-filled night sky. And now here was this stranger telling me the same thing.

"You and your dog had a different relationship than most people have with their animals," she told me. "You were like a guardian to him; someone he chose to live his life with to help him evolve."

My mind raced and I could hardly hear what the woman was saying, because at the time I was a spokesperson for the Guardian Campaign at In Defense of Animals.

"Your dog had a purpose in this life, and you let him fulfill it by giving him your love," she said. "He wants you to know that he is happy, and grateful that you saved him, and he's in the stars watching over you."

I barely remember eating my lunch, driving home, or anything else that happened that day. The green-eyed tarot card reader had tapped into something that I had not put into words before that moment, but I now realized was true. I believe animals are here for their own purposes, for their own self-actualization, and for their own evolution. It is no coincidence that we choose each other in this lifetime. I chose a six-pack, and they chose me. Their love changed me in ways that I cannot fully describe in this book and am eternally grateful for. Together, we helped one another become healthier, happier, and just a little more extraordinary. Their gifts are what I will take with me . . . beyond this existence and into forever.

Afterword

Our cats and dogs have lived beside us for thousands of years. Throughout time, they have protected and cared for us. Today they are ensuring our survival through our most important asset: our health and well-being.

From friendship to service, our cats and dogs are there for us with a dedication and love that is second to none. But are we there for them?

Approximately 7.6 million animal companions enter shelters every year. Of those, approximately 3.9 million are dogs and 3.4 million are cats. Each year, nearly 2.7 million animals are euthanized. The suffering of one cat or dog is heart-wrenching for an animal lover; the anguish of so many is unbearable. Our cat and dog friends deserve more from us. We are their protectors, their guardians, and their friends. So when it comes to your animals, please abide by these three principles:

1. Adopt, don't shop.
2. Be a guardian, not an owner.
3. Nurture your animal–human partnerships daily.

Whichever animal companion you have the fortune to live beside, whether it's a cat, dog, horse, pot-bellied pig, cow, lizard, or lamb, know that you are privileged and blessed to be in the company of angels.

Together, may you and your animal friends live a healthy, happy, and extraordinary life!

Notes

1. National Council on Aging, "Healthy Aging Facts." https://www.ncoa.org/news/resources-for-reporters/get-the-facts/healthy-aging-facts.

2. Erika Friedmann *et al.*, "Pet's Presence and Owner's Blood Pressures during the Daily Lives of Pet Owners with Pre- to Mild Hypertension." *Anthrozoös* 26, no. 4 (2015): 535-550.

3. C.J. Charnetski, S. Riggers, & F.X. Brennan. "Effect of petting a dog on immune system function." *Psychological Reports* 95 (2004): 1087–1091. doi: 10.2466/pr0.95.3f.1087-1091.

4. Brad Kollus, "The Power of Petting" (November 2011). http://www.thecatsite.com/a/the-power-of-petting.

5. Elizabeth Deffner, "Heat-generating dogs treat fibromyalgia pain in humans." *Natural News*, June 23, 2006. http://www.naturalnews.com/019458_therapeutic_pets_fibromyalgia.html#.

6. E. Muggenthaler, "The felid purr: A healing mechanism?" *Proceedings of the 12th International Conference on Low Frequency Noise and Vibration and Its Control* (Bristol, UK: 2006). http://www.animalvoice.com/catpurrP.htm.

7. T.F. Cook, "The relief of dyspnoea in cats by purring." *New Zealand Veterinary Journal*, 21 (2006): 53–54. doi: 10.1080/00480169.1973.34076.

8. Ken Tudor, "Pet 'Kisses': Health Hazard or Health Benefit?" *PetMD*, January 2014. http://www.petmd.com/blogs/thedailyvet/ktudor/2014/jan/are-dog-licks-unhealthy-for-people-31207.

9. Kevin Behan, *Your Dog is Your Mirror: The Emotional Capacity of Our Dogs and Ourselves* (Novato, CA: New World Library, 2011).

10. D. Yuhas, "Pets: Why Do We Have Them?" *Scientific American* 24, no. 3 (December 2015): 10.

11. C. Del Percio *et al.*, "'Neural efficiency' of athletes' brain for upright standing: A high-resolution EEG study." *Brain Research Bulletin* 79, no. 3–4 (2009): 193–200. doi: 10.1016/j.brainresbull.2009.02.001.

12. N. Martin, "Michael Jaco Interview: Former Navy Seal And Author Of 'The Intuitive Warrior'" (2014). https://www.goodreads.com/author_blog_posts/5560500-michael-jaco-interview-former-navy-seal-and-author-of-the-intuitive-wa.

13. Jon Gordon, *The No Complaining Rule: Positive Ways to Deal with Negativity at Work* (Hoboken, NJ: John Wiley & Sons, 2008).

14. Alice G. Walton, "How Much Sugar Are Americans Eating?" *Forbes*, August 30, 2012. http://www.forbes.com/sites/alicegwalton/2012/08/30/how-much-sugar-are-americans-eating-infographic/#49a2bdc61f71.

15. Veterinary Practice News, "Report: Chronic Disease Grows With Pets' Waists" (May 2012). http://www.veterinarypracticenews.com/May-2012/Report-Chronic-Disease-Grows-With-Pets-Waists.

16. John Ericson, "75% of Americans May Suffer From Chronic Dehydration, According to Doctors." *Medical Daily*, July 3, 2013. http://www.medicaldaily.com/75-americans-may-suffer-chronic-dehydration-according-doctors-247393.

17. Peter F. Cook *et al.*, "Awake Canine fMRI Predicts Dogs' Preference for Praise Versus Food." *Social Cognitive and Affective Neuroscience* (August 2016). doi: 10.1093/scan/nsw102.

18. *Forks over Knives*, directed by Lee Fulkerson (Virgil Films and Entertainment, October 2013), DVD.

19. Thomas Campbell, MD, "Masai and Inuit High-Protein Diets: A Closer Look." Center for Nutrition Studies (July 17, 2015; modified May 3, 2016). http://nutritionstudies.org/masai-and-inuit-high-protein-diets-a-closer-look.

20. Dan Buettner, "Reverse Engineering Longevity." *Blue Zones*, April 9, 2014. https://www.bluezones.com/2014/04/power-9.

21. E.S. Paul, "Empathy with animals and with humans: are they linked?" *Anthrozoös* 13, no. 4 (2000): 194–202. doi: 10.2752/089279300786999699.

22. People for the Ethical Treatment of Animals (PETA), "Vegans Save 198 Animals a Year" (December 13, 2010). http://www.peta.org/blog/vegans-save-185-animals-year.

23. Darren E.R. Warburton, Crystal Whitney Nicol, & Shannon S.D. Bredin, "Health benefits of physical activity: the evidence." *Canadian Medical Association Journal* 174, no.6 (2006): 801–809. doi: 10.1503/cmaj.051351.

24. Leandro Fórnias Machado Rezende et al., "All-Cause Mortality Attributable to Sitting Time: Analysis of 54 Countries Worldwide." *American Journal of Preventive Medicine* 51, no. 2 (August 2016): 253–263. doi: 10.1016/j.amepre.2016.01.022.

25. Hayley E. Cutt, Matthew W. Knuiman, and Billie Giles-Corti, "Does getting a dog increase recreational walking?" *International Journal of Behavioral Nutrition and Physical Activity* 5, no. 1 (2008): 1. doi: 10.1186/1479-5868-5-17.

26. "10,000 steps may not be enough." The Associated Press, February 9, 2004. http://www.nbcnews.com/id/4221278/ns/health/t/steps-may-not-be-enough/#.V8S2aIXzTMA.

27. Jason Cody & Mathew Reeves, "Dog walkers more likely to reach exercise benchmarks." *MSU Today,* March 10, 2011. http://msutoday.msu.edu/news/2011/dog-walkers-more-likely-to-reach-exercise-benchmarks/.

28. Ibid.

29. Lisa Wood et al., "The Pet Factor: Companion Animals as a Conduit for Getting to Know People, Friendship Formation and Social Support." *PLoS ONE* 10, no. 4 (2015). doi: 10.1371/journal.pone.0122085.

30. Adit A. Ginde, Mark C. Liu, and Carlos A. Camargo, "Demographic Differences and Trends of Vitamin D Insufficiency in the US Population, 1988-2004." *Archives of Internal Medicine* 169, no. 6 (2009): 626-632. doi: 10.1001/archinternmed.2008.604.

31. Centers for Disease Control (CDC), "Insufficient Sleep Is a Public Health Problem" (September 3, 2015). http://www.cdc.gov/features/dssleep.

32. Ann M. Williamson & Anne-Marie Feyer, "Moderate sleep deprivation produces impairments in cognitive and motor performance equivalent to legally prescribed levels of alcohol intoxication." *Occupational & Environmental Medicine* 57, no. 10 (October 2000): 649–655. doi: 10.1136/oem.57.10.649.

33. Jing Zhang *et al.,* "Extended Wakefulness: Compromised Metabolics in and Degeneration of Locus Ceruleus Neurons." *The Journal of Neuroscience* 34, no. 12 (March 2014): 4418–4431. doi: 10.1523/JNEUROSCI.5025-12.2014

34. Camille Peri, "10 Things to Hate About Sleep Loss." WebMD (February 2014). Retrieved from http://www.webmd.com/sleep-disorders/features/10-results-sleep-loss.

35. Sharon Guynup, "Light Pollution Taking Toll on Wildlife, Eco-Groups Say." *National Geographic Today* (April 17, 2003). http://news.nationalgeographic.com/news/2003/04/0417_030417_tvlightpollution.html.

36. Florida Fish and Wildlife Conservation Commission, "Artificial Lighting and Sea Turtle Hatchling Behavior." http://myfwc.com/research/wildlife/sea-turtles/threats/artificial-lighting.

37. Guynup, "Light Pollution."

38. Shelley S. Tworoger *et al.*, "Effects of a Yearlong Moderate-Intensity Exercise and a Stretching Intervention on Sleep Quality in Postmenopausal Women." SLEEP-NEW YORK THEN WESTCHESTER- 26, no. 7 (November 2003): 830–836. http://www.ncbi.nlm.nih.gov/pubmed/14655916.

39. Harvard Mental Health Letter, "Yoga for anxiety and depression" (April 2009). http://www.health.harvard.edu/mind-and-mood/yoga-for-anxiety-and-depression.

40. Karen B. London, "Where Does Your Dog Sleep?" *The Bark* (December 23, 2011). http://thebark.com/content/where-does-your-dog-sleep.

41. Tara Parker-Pope, "Learning While You Dream." *The New York Times*, April 22, 2010. http://well.blogs.nytimes.com/2010/04/22/learning-while-you-dream/?_r=0.

42. Twila Tardif *et al.*, "Baby's first 10 words." *Developmental Psychology* 44, no. 4 (July 2008): 929–938. doi: 10.1037/0012-1649.44.4.929.

43. Edward O. Wilson, *Biophilia* (Cambridge: Harvard University Press, 1984).

44. Centers for Disease Control and Prevention (CDC), "Childhood Obesity Facts" (August 27, 2015). https://www.cdc.gov/healthyschools/obesity/facts.htm.

45. Centers for Disease Control and Prevention (CDC), "Autism and Developmental Disabilities Monitoring (ADDM) Network" (July 29, 2016). http://www.cdc.gov/ncbddd/autism/addm.html.

46. Ganesa Wegienka *et al.*, "Lifetime dog and cat exposure and dog- and cat-specific sensitization at age 18 years." *Clinical & Experimental Allergy* 41, no. 7 (June 2011): 979–986. doi: 10.1111/j.1365-2222.2011.03747.x.

47. Eija Bergroth *et al.*, "Respiratory Tract Illnesses During the First Year of Life: Effect of Dog and Cat Contacts." *Pediatrics* 130, no. 2 (August 2012). doi: 10.1542/peds.2011-2825.

48. American Heart Association, "Overweight in Children" (July 5, 2016). http://www.heart.org/HEARTORG/HealthyLiving/HealthyKids/ChildhoodObesity/Overweight-in-Children_UCM_304054_Article.jsp#.V8XJooXzTMB.

49. Anne M. Gadomski *et al.*, "Pet Dogs and Children's Health: Opportunities for Chronic Disease Prevention?" *Preventing Chronic Disease* 12 (November 2015). doi: 10.5888/pcd12.150204.

50. Christopher G. Owen *et al.*, "Family Dog Ownership and Levels of Physical Activity in Childhood: Findings From the Child Heart and Health Study in England." *American Journal of Public Health* 100, no. 9 (September 2010): 1669–1671. doi: 10.2105/AJPH.2009.188193.

51. Lynn M. Hayner, "The Amazing Human and Dog Bond." *Dog Fancy*, January 2013. https://www.waltham.com/news/waltham-in-january-edition-of-dog-fancy.shtml.

52. Martin H. Smith & Cheryl Meehan, "Canine buddies help youth develop reading skills." University of California Division of Agriculture and Natural Resources. http://ucanr.edu/delivers/categories/?impact=800&delivers=1.

53. Francesca Di Meglio, "Stress Takes Its Toll on College Students." *Bloomberg*, May 10, 2012. http://www.bloomberg.com/news/articles/2012-05-10/stress-takes-its-toll-on-college-students.

54. Julian Aiken, "Meet Monty." *Yale Law School News & Blogs*, September 19, 2012. http://library.law.yale.edu/news/meet-monty.

55. Olivia Pittman, "20 Pet-Friendly College Campuses." *College Raptor.* https://www.collegeraptor.com/blog/on-campus/20-pet-friendly-college-campuses

56. Kia Kokalitcheva, "Here Are the 12 Most Pet-Friendly Companies." *Fortune*, March 8, 2016. http://fortune.com/2016/03/08/here-are-the-12-most-pet-friendly-companies

57. Randolph T. Barker *et al.*, "Preliminary investigation of employee's dog presence on stress and organizational perceptions." *International Journal of Workplace Health Management* 5, no. 1 (2012): 15–30. doi: 10.1108/17538351211215366.

58. Wendy Wang, Kim Parker, & Paul Taylor, "Breadwinner Moms." Pew Research Center, May 29, 2013. http://www.pewsocialtrends.org/2013/05/29/breadwinner-moms.

59. V. Vaccarino, A. Towfighi, & S. Oertelt-Prigione, "News release." *Archives of Internal Medicine,* vol. 169 (October 2009).

60. Centers for Disease Control and Prevention (CDC), "Leading Causes of Death in Females" (July 2015). http://www.cdc.gov/women/lcod.

61. Edward Archer *et al.*, "Maternal Inactivity: 45-Year Trends in Mothers' Use of Time." *Mayo Clinic Proceedings* 88, no. 12 (December 2013): 1368–1377. doi: 10.1016/j.mayocp.2013.09.009.

62. Carri Westgarth *et al.*, "Dog Ownership during Pregnancy, Maternal Activity, and Obesity: A Cross-Sectional Study." *PLoS one* 7, no. 2 (February 2012). e31315. doi:10.1371/journal.pone.0031315.

63. Mats Hammar & Richard Lindgren, "Does physical exercise influence the frequency of postmenopausal hot flushes?" *Acta Obstetricia et Gynecologica Scandinavica* 69, no. 5 (1990): 409–412. doi: 10.1016/0378-5122(91)90234-H.

64. Pets Are Wonderful Support, "The Health Benefits of Companion Animals"

(2007). https://www.nps.gov/goga/learn/management/upload/Comment-4704-attachment_.pdf.

65. Lois Baker, "Pet Dog Or Cat Controls Blood Pressure Better Than ACE Inhibitor, UB Study Of Stockbrokers Finds." University at Buffalo News Center, November 7, 1999. http://www.buffalo.edu/news/releases/1999/11/4489.html.

66. Centers for Disease Control and Prevention (CDC), "Leading Causes of Death in Males United States, 2013" (July 13, 2015). http://www.cdc.gov/men/lcod/2013/index.htm.

67. U.S. Census Bureau, "Sixty-five plus in the United States" (May 1995). https://www.census.gov/population/socdemo/statbriefs/agebrief.html.

68. Parminder Raina *et al.*, "Influence of Companion Animals on the Physical and Psychological Health of Older People: An Analysis of a One-Year Longitudinal Study." *Journal of the American Geriatrics Society* 47, no. 3 (March 1999): 323–329. doi:10.1111/j.1532-5415.1999.tb02996.x.

69. "Meals on Wheels helps feed pets of seniors, disabled." The Associated Press, December 25, 2013. http://www.cbsnews.com/news/meals-on-wheels-helps-feed-pets-of-seniors-disabled.

70. Tara Parker-Pope, "Forget the Treadmill. Get a Dog." *The New York Times*, March 14, 2011. http://well.blogs.nytimes.com/2011/03/14/forget-the-treadmill-get-a-dog/?_r=0.

71. Lynette A. Hart, Benjamin L. Hart, and Bonita L. Bergin, "Socializing Effects of Service Dogs for People with Disabilities." *Anthrozoös* 1, no. 1 (January 1987): 41–44. doi: 10.2752/089279388787058696.

72. Pamela Carlisle-Frank & Joshua M. Frank, "Owners, guardians, and owner-guardians: Differing relationships with pets." *Anthrozoös* 19, no. 3 (2006): 225–242. doi: 10.2752/089279306785415574.

73. ASPCA. "Pet Statistics." http://www.aspca.org/animal-homelessness/shelter-intake-and-surrender/pet-statistics.

74. Adam Gorlick, "Media multitaskers pay mental price, Stanford study shows." *Stanford News*, August 24, 2009. http://news.stanford.edu/2009/08/24/multitask-research-study-082409.

75. Travis Bradberry, "Multitasking Damages Your Brain And Career, New Studies Suggest." *Forbes*, October 8, 2014. http://www.forbes.com/sites/travisbradberry/2014/10/08/multitasking-damages-your-brain-and-career-new-studies-suggest/#2e59699e2c16.

76. HelpGuide. "Benefits of Mindfulness." Adapted from a Harvard Health Publications report. http://www.helpguide.org/harvard/benefits-of-mindfulness.htm

77. Bret Stetka, "Changing Our DNA through Mind Control?" *Scientific American*, December 16, 2014. http://www.scientificamerican.com/article/changing-our-dna-through-mind-control.

78. Steve Sisgold, *Whole Body Intelligence: Get Out of Your Head and Into Your Body to Achieve Greater Wisdom, Confidence, and Success* (Emmaus, PA: Rodale Books, 2015).

79. James Clear, "How Long Does It Actually Take to Form a New Habit? (Backed by Science)." *The Huffington Post*, April 10, 2014. http://www.huffingtonpost.com/james-clear/forming-new-habits_b_5104807.html.

80. The American Institute of Stress. "America's #1 Health Problem." http://www.stress.org/americas-1-health-problem.

81. Andrew Newberg & Mark Robert Waldman, *Words Can Change Your Brain* (New York: Penguin, 2012).

82. Masaru Emoto, *Messages from Water and the Universe* (Carlsbad, CA: Hay House, 2010).

83. Jennifer Viegas, "Dogs understand us better than chimps do, scientists say." *NBC News*, February 8, 2012. http://www.nbcnews.com/id/46319430/ns/technology_ and_science-science/t/dogs-understand-us-better-chimps-do-scientists-say/#. V8Xi54XzTMB.

84. Kevin Behan, *Your Dog is Your Mirror: The Emotional Capacity of Our Dogs and Ourselves* (Novato, CA: New World Library, 2011).

85. Ingrid King, "Your Stress is Impacting Your Cat's Health." *Animal Wellness*. http://animalwellnessmagazine.com/stress-impacting-your-cats-health.

86. Daniel Goleman, *Emotional Intelligence: Why it Can Matter More than IQ* (New York: Bantam, 1995).

87. Karine Silva, Joana Bessa, and Liliana de Sousa, "Auditory contagious yawning in domestic dogs (*Canis familiaris*): first evidence for social modulation." *Animal Cognition* 15, no. 4 (2012): 721-724. doi: 10.1007/s10071-012-0473-2.

88. Joseph Campbell & Bill Moyers, *The Power of Myth* (New York: Anchor Books, 1991).

89. Alina Tugend, "Tiptoeing Out of One's Comfort Zone (and of Course, Back In)." *The New York Times*, February 11, 2011. http://www.nytimes.com/2011/02/12/ yourmoney/12shortcuts.html.

90. Wikipedia. "Personal life of Leonardo da Vinci." https://en.wikipedia.org/wiki/ Personal_life_of_Leonardo_da_Vinci.

91. Stanley Coren, *The Pawprints of History: Dogs and the Course of Human Events* (New York: Atria Books, 2003).

92. Summer Anne Burton, "16 Brilliant Artists And Their Animal Muses." *Buzzfeed*, August 23, 2012. https://www.buzzfeed.com/summeranne/16-brilliant-artists-and-their-animal-muses?utm_term=.kiXlnP7nl#.fo7lqLYql.

93. Stanley Coren, "Dogs, Cats, Classical Music, and Frederic Chopin." *Psychology Today*, December 20, 2012. https://www.psychologytoday.com/blog/canine-corner/201212/dogs-cats-classical-music-and-fr-d-ric-chopin.

94. Rachel Moss, "How To Find Love: Study Suggests Dog Walking Helps Brits Meet Partners And Lifelong Friends." *The Huffington Post*, June 25, 2015. http://www.huffingtonpost.co.uk/2015/06/25/dog-walking-meet-people-relationships_n_7661090.html.

95. Stanley Coren, "Health and Psychological Benefits of Bonding with a Pet Dog." *Psychology Today*, June 7, 2009. https://www.psychologytoday.com/blog/canine-corner/200906/health-and-psychological-benefits-bonding-pet-dog.

96. Lisa J. Wood *et al.*, "More than a furry companion: The ripple effect of companion animals on neighborhood interactions and sense of community." *Society & Animals* 15, no. 1 (2007): 43–56. doi: 10.1163/156853007X169333

97. Lorie Johnson, "The Deadly Consequences of Unforgiveness." *CBN News*, June 2015. http://www1.cbn.com/cbnnews/healthscience/2015/June/The-Deadly-Consequences-of-Unforgiveness.

98. Therese A. Rando, *Grief, Dying and Death: Clinical Interventions for Caregivers* (Champaign, IL: Research Press, 1984).

99. Bronnie Ware, *The Top Five Regrets of the Dying: A Life Transformed by the Dearly Departing* (Carlsbad, CA: Hay House, 2012).

100. Author unknown.

101. Deepak Chopra, "Deepak Chopra: What I've Learned About Love." eHarmony. http://www.eharmony.com/dating-advice/about-you/deepak-chopra-what-ive-learned-about-love.

102. Alice Park, "The 100 Most Influential People: Robert Lanza." *TIME*, April 23, 2014. http://time.com/72173/robert-lanza-2014-time-100.

103. Robert Lanza & Bob Berman, *Biocentrism: How Life and Consciousness are the Keys to Understanding the True Nature of the Universe* (Dallas, TX: BenBella Books, 2010).

Acknowledgments

I wish to thank the following people for their contributions, inspiration, and support in helping me create this book:

My husband, Ken Fischer, whose unwavering support, a mind for great ideas, and uncanny ways to get me laughing make me think I must have won the cosmic lottery to end up with a guy like him.

Giulia Notari, my illustrator extraordinaire, who added an unexpected and greatly appreciated dimension of wonder to my words. Krissa Lagos, my editor, made the arduous easy. I could not have done this without her.

The following individuals shared their stories of connection, joy, and loss. I am honored by their trust in me to tell their stories: Dr. Ulka Agarwal, Peter Ashendon, Diane B., Michelle Bechtol, Constance Blake, Leanne Buttles, Michelle Cehn, Karen Cleff, Julia Clements, Danny Colter, Laura Cottingham, Robert Crane, Thomas Dellaira, Jacob Fries, Anne Marie Goop, Jeffrey Ho, Beth Jackson, Susan Johnson, Steve Kehrli, Pamela Kimmel, Christine Kloser, Tanya Masterson, Sandie McCall, Cindy Moran, Stephanie Neighbor, Jill Robinson, Jojo Soriano, Marie Thomas, Cynthia Travaglio, Linda Trenholm, and 8.

A big thanks to my beta readers who scoured my book's pages and improved them in countless ways—especially Charity Goodin, Malia MacKillop, and Elisa Montes De Oca, who read the manuscript from beginning to end and took their jobs "very seriously."

Special thanks to Jack Canfield, Neal Barnard, M.D., Ingrid Newkirk, Dr. Elliot Katz, Sheryl Matthys, W. Bruce Cameron, Jackson Galaxy, Jane Velez Mitchell, Gary Rydstrom, Karen Gulmon, and Pen Pals for their contributions.

To Steve Harrison and all of my Quantum Leap coaches—especially Geoffrey Berwind and Martha Bullen—thank you for your gentle guidance on my many leaps through authorship.

To Michael Friel for his superb photographic eye and Cindy Moran for her makeup expertise. Both created magic on photo shoot day.

To my stepchildren, Greg and Gina, and their spouses, Yolanda and Helio—there is nothing more beautiful than laughing with you, enjoying a good game of cornhole, and knowing that you are my family.

To Sarah M., who taught me that to be a good pack leader one must first be a benevolent leader. I have not forgotten.

And finally, to Cody, Jester, Teddy, Roxy, Rudy, and Dakota, my six-pack of cats and dogs—rescues who have returned this small kindness with steadfast friendship, unconditional love, and the inspiration for this book. I definitely got the better deal.

About the Author

photo © Michael Fried

Carlyn Montes De Oca is an animal-human health expert, author, speaker, plant-based nutritional consultant, and acupuncturist. She holds a bachelor's degree from Loyola Marymount University in communication arts and a master's degree in Traditional Chinese Medicine from Emperor's College. She is also certified in plant-based nutrition from the T. Colin Campbell Center for Nutritional Studies at Cornell University. Montes De Oca was voted PETA's Sexiest Vegetarian Over 50 and has been a spokesperson for the Guardian Campaign at In Defense of Animals. She is also the founder of The Animal-Human Health Connection, which focuses on bringing awareness to the many powerful ways that animals enhance human health, happiness, and longevity. Montes De Oca lives in Marin County with her husband, Ken, and her beloved rescue animals. For more information, go to www.AnimalHumanHealth.com.

Selected Titles from She Writes Press

She Writes Press is an independent publishing company founded to serve women writers everywhere. Visit us at www.shewritespress.com.

Note to Self: A Seven-Step Path to Gratitude and Growth by Laurie Buchanan. $16.95, 978-1-63152-113-3. Transforming intention into action, *Note to Self* equips you to shed your baggage, bridging the gap between where you are and where you want to be—body, mind, and spirit—and empowering you to step into joy-filled living *now!*

Stop Giving it Away: How to Stop Self-Sacrificing and Start Claiming Your Space, Power, and Happiness by Cherilynn Veland. $16.95, 978-1-63152-958-0. An empowering guide designed to help women break free from the trappings of the needs, wants, and whims of other people—and the self-imposed limitations that are keeping them from happiness.

Think Better. Live Better. 5 Steps to Create the Life You Deserve by Francine Huss. $16.95, 978-1-938314-66-7. With the help of this guide, readers will learn to cultivate more creative thoughts, realign their mindset, and gain a new perspective on life.

The Art of Play: Igniting Your Imagination to Unlock Insight, Healing, and Joy by Joan Stanford. $19.95, 978-1-63152-030-3. Lifelong "non-artist" Joan Stanford shares the creative process that led her to insight and healing, and shares ways for others to do the same.

The Clarity Effect: How Being More Present Can Transform Your Work and Life by Sarah Harvey Yao. $16.95, 978-1-63152-958-0. A practical, strategy-filled guide for stressed professionals looking for clarity, strength, and joy in their work and home lives.

The Thriver's Edge: Seven Keys to Transform the Way You Live, Love, and Lead by Donna Stoneham. $16.95, 978-1-63152-980-1. A "coach in a book" from master executive coach and leadership expert Dr. Donna Stoneham, *The Thriver's Edge* outlines a practical road map to breaking free of the barriers keeping you from being everything you're capable of being.